# The College Search Simplified

## A Step By Step Guide to Finding and Applying to Colleges

Christine Tuccille Merry

ISBN-13: 978-1-7980-3298-5

# DEDICATION

This book is dedicated to my wonderful husband, Jim, and my sons, Jasper and Hugo, who provide me with infinite opportunities to do research.

# CONTENTS

# INTRODUCTION

Like most parents, as I embarked on the college search with my oldest son, I felt overwhelmed with how to even begin. What kinds of schools are out there? What kinds of schools will my son get into? How will we ever afford it?

I bought a couple of college guides and started reading about various schools, looking for details that would jump out at me as things he would like. "Oh, the campus is an arboretum! He'd love that," I would think, or, "very accessible professors and small classes, that sounds good." Then I'd glance at the cost and see that the tuition for most private schools is $50,000 or more. When combined with room, board, and other fees the cost of attendance could climb to $70,000 or more. Per year.

I felt truly stumped at first. Should we only consider our in-state schools? Would we get any financial aid? If so, how much? And, who actually gets academic merit scholarships? How do you apply for them?

Thanks to the Internet and books, there is a lot of information out there, but it's not all in one place. So I started doing a lot of research. I found many really helpful sites. I attended countless webinars about how to navigate and understand the college selection process. I read books. I talked with friends who recently went through this process with their kids.

After doing all this research, I decided to create a blog as a place to compile all the information, so I could refer back to it and also so I could share it with my friends. Of course there is always more to know, but I got to a point when I felt I had found as much information as I possibly could to make really informed decisions regarding the college application process. My son has now sent in all his applications, has begun hearing back, and we are learning that all this research paid off since he is getting the results we expected.

I decided to further organize this information and share it with more families by putting it together in an easy-to-navigate book. One reason I decided to create the book was frustration about the whole process, and more than a touch of cynicism. If we are expected to spend so much money on higher education, why are so many people confused about the process and mystified about which kids gain access to which institutions? Why are teenagers so stressed about getting the "right" test scores or participating in the "right" activities? Why do colleges and universities hold so much power over the future of our children and our bank accounts?

I am hoping that reading this short book will allow you to eliminate all the hours spread out over several years that I put into my research. You might still need to look up information specific to your child, but these pages should cut down on searching for the bulk of information that is relevant to almost everyone.

I hope you find it useful! Good luck.

Christine Merry

## HOW TO USE THIS BOOK

I refer to online articles, websites, and books in many of the chapters. If you would like to read more, please refer to the bibliography and resources sections at the end of the book.

# SECTION 1 WHAT KIND OF A STUDENT ARE YOU?

## CHAPTER 1
## EACH STUDENT IS A PUZZLE PIECE

I have come to view each student undergoing the college search as a unique puzzle piece looking for the puzzle to which he or she belongs. There isn't one list of great schools to which everyone should apply and hope to gain admission. There are many great schools that offer fine educations, and it's important to find a place where your student can thrive.

The first thing I would recommend you do is buy one or two college guides that include a lot of helpful information. Two good examples are the *Fiske Guide to Colleges* (Fiske, 2018) and *The Princeton Review Guide to Colleges* (Franek, O'Toole and Soto 2017). Both books contain such information as the size of schools, acceptance rates, descriptions of strong departments and popular majors at the school, descriptions of the students and atmosphere, financial aid policies, SAT scores and GPAs of the middle 50%

of accepted students, and more. Both guides come out with a new edition every year. Your local library may carry them, so you can take a look before buying them.

The hard part, of course, even if you have a guide, is where to start. Ideally, parents and students who are planning on college after high school should begin thinking about college in 9th or 10th grade. At this stage, parents and students can talk to friends or family members who have already done a college search—this is particularly useful if you know older kids who have similar strengths and interests—and see where they looked and applied. You can also visit a few schools that are close by that are very different from one another, for example a large state university, a mid-size school, and a small college (if you don't live near any institutions of higher learning, many schools offer virtual tours on their websites). This can be done very informally—you can begin by walking around the campus, or you can sign up for an information session and tour to get a better feel for the place. This way your child can begin to get an idea of what type environment he or she prefers.

Although most students won't yet have opinions about some items on the following list, there are many things that parents and students can begin thinking about early on:

- Close to home or far away?
- Rural, small town, or large city?
- Small, medium, or large school?
- Student body: What are the students like? What types of students thrive here?
- Strengths and weaknesses of various departments and programs.
- Cost.

The first two categories are pretty self-explanatory. Is the student willing to attend college more than a few hours' drive away (and do the parents support this)? How about a flight away? Does the student have a preference for a rural or urban location? Giving some thought to location now can make it easier later to create a list of schools to consider.

Next, a student can give some thought to whether she would prefer a large or small school. This is where visiting those nearby campuses can be helpful. If your child feels claustrophobic on a small campus or overwhelmed on a large one, you can at least narrow your search to certain sized schools.

The next item on the list is really important when reading potential schools in the guides. Pay attention to descriptions of the s body! I have come across many contradictory adjectives and phrase could make a student feel like he found a home or like he found a place he would never want to step foot. Some opposing examples I've come across: "pointy" vs. "well-rounded" students, "need to be assertive to be noticed here" vs. "professors are very accessible," "activist" vs. "not political," "strong school spirit" vs. "no school spirit." Sometimes there are other telling descriptors of the students, "the last bastion of the southern gentleman," or "intellectual," etc.

You can look for other details in college guides that might help your child determine whether a school could be a good fit. Do you have to be part of the Greek system to have a social life? Is the library always packed, including on Saturday nights? I'm continually amazed when I hear about kids who are considering schools with very different student bodies. It's hard to imagine the same kid being equally happy at a school where the social life is dominated by a huge party scene and Greek life, and at another school where there is no Greek life or many parties. And, it's hard to imagine the same kid being as happy where students are described as "off-beat and weird" at one school and "preppy and conventional" at the other.

The next item on the list, "evaluating the strengths and weaknesses of various departments," may be an item that needs to be put on hold if your child has no idea about college major. However, if you have a child who has some idea of what he or she would like to study, great! Once you get a general idea of size and location of school, you can begin to research specific departments. Take a look at how many full time professors there are in that department, and how many classes are offered. Find out whether the classes are all offered every year. It's also worth spending a little time finding out about research opportunities for undergraduates in that department, and any other opportunities such as internships. These websites can be helpful places to ask questions about various schools, and read reviews about departments and experiences: www.collegeconfidential.com and http://www.niche.com.

And now the final item on the list, cost. It's an important one, so maybe it should have been first! One rule of thumb is to not let your child apply to a school you cannot afford. This makes sense to me, but I found it difficult to determine which schools would be affordable in the long run as most of the price tags are really high. I go more in depth about the determining the cost of college in Chapter 12, "How Much Is College Going to Cost?" This is such an important consideration, I would highly recommend spending time on this topic. There are a lot of sad stories out there about kids who had their hopes dashed because their dream schools were just too expensive. An excellent website with very in-depth analysis of college costs is www.thecollegesolution.com, run by Lynn O'Shaughnessy.

With any luck, developing this list will help your child figure out the types of schools where he or she can thrive. Maybe she'll realize that she wants a mid-size school with division III sports and lots of school spirit, undergraduate research opportunities, and that is within a five-hour drive from home. That's not a bad starting point! Now you just need to find some places where your unique puzzle piece will fit.

# CHAPTER 2
## WELL-ROUNDED VS. POINTY

Part of figuring out what kind of (college) puzzle will be the right place for an individual (student) piece is figuring out what type of student you are and in which schools that type of student can thrive.

Most people are familiar with the concept of a well-rounded student. This is someone who is good at and involved with many things: the excellent student who is also an athlete, sings in a choir, is a member of the robotics team, and although it is often not stated, I think it is usually implied that this person is also very good socially. This person is often "popular." I think many people think that this type of student is what "colleges are looking for" and many students try to force themselves into this mold. Many parents try to push their kids into this mold because they think it will help them. But, trying to become someone you're not, most of us know, can lead to misery.

So, what is a "pointy" student? Most people are less familiar with this concept. This is a student who is definitely not well-rounded. This is the student who has specific passions and talents and wants to spend most of his time developing these intense areas of interest. The pointy student is not interested in spreading himself too thin. This student, depending on his area of interest, might be referred to as a nerd. What do colleges think of these students?

Surprise! Well, maybe it's not a surprise. It turns out that most selective colleges love these students. Using the "major admissions criteria" and "ideal student" sections as a guide in the book, *The Hidden Ivies* (Greene and Greene, 2016), this is what some schools have to say:

"The 'perfect 4.0 GPA student 'is not always our primary pick, especially if he or she were achievement oriented largely to match their parents' expectations rather than intrinsically motivated to learn. The student who thrives best here generally has obvious 'edges' rather than being perfectly well-rounded." (Recent dean at University of Rochester).

"Those who do best are 'Intellectual students who have a deep passion for anything—from interests in lacrosse to track to science fiction to computer technology to politics to philosophy.'" (Graduating Senior at Swarthmore).

"That's why, in selecting each incoming class, we look beyond the stereotypical 'well-rounded student.' Instead, we look for those who bring a mix of passions, eccentricities, and ambitions to create a well-rounded campus community." (Williams College).

"...serious about their academic career, intellectually curious, hardworking, desiring to be stimulated by demanding faculty..." "Chicago is not a setting in which to hang out or do enough to get by and feel part of the mainstream." (University of Chicago).

"Anyone who loves what they do will do well here. You have to have a passion for something and Kenyon fosters those passions." (Students at Kenyon College).

In addition to information found in *The Hidden Ivies* (Greene and Greene, 2016), most information sessions I attended with my son at various colleges mentioned the importance of students developing their unique talents and areas of interest (in fact, I think I learned the term "pointy" from an information session at Swarthmore). They want exceptional students who have really achieved in an area (or two) of focus more than they want someone who is pretty good at lots of things. Overall, they want the incoming student body to be well-rounded, but not the individual students—they hope that each student stands out in a different way.

For a really in-depth look at what Ivy League schools are looking for, I always refer to the article, *"How to Get Into Harvard and the Ivy League, by a Harvard Alum,"* (Cheng, Allen, 2018) of Prep Scholar. The author uses the term "spike" instead of "point," but it's the same thing.

"That's great," you might say, "but, what if my kid really is naturally well-rounded?" There is good news here too. Some schools do seem to be composed of students who are generally more well-rounded. From the "ideal student" section in *The Hidden Ivies* (Greene and Greene, 2016):

"An outgoing personality and interest in either or both athletics and community service are important to finding a place within the community. An interest in Greek life is a plus for many students." (Bucknell University).

"Smart, hardworking, ambitious, community-oriented, confident, self-initiating, and independent are the requisite qualities. Almost as important is the student's EQ (emotional intelligence) and social skills. Duke is a hyperactive social environment, one that calls for the ability to maneuver one's way through myriad clubs, activities, internships, fraternities and sororities, teams, and residential-life challenges and opportunities." (Duke University).

"Attracts those interested in a more unified collegiate experience, with a lot of school spirit and a strong sense of community. Athletic students, and those inclined to cheer on their friends, will fit in well here." (Holy Cross).

"Students should be outgoing and assertive, and willing to take some part in guiding their own studies...a student who likes to play sports as well as cheer on friends on the field will enjoy weekend life here. Dickinson likes smart, motivated, friendly, earnest, and idealistic students." (Dickinson College).

It is obvious from the above statements that different schools value different types of students. The benefit to being "pointy" is that these students stand out. Their applications will be unique, and they are likely to have shown high achievement in particular areas that can be very attractive to colleges. According to experts at www.collegevine.com, colleges like students who have excelled in focused areas because they have already proven themselves to be people who can apply themselves and achieve.

They are likely to continue to be successful and high achieving in college and after they graduate, which will reflect very well on these schools.

Many of the schools that prefer pointy students will still end up admitting many well-rounded students, because there are more well-rounded students in the applicant pool. The challenge for these students is that they are harder to distinguish from other well-rounded students, unless they stand out in some way. However, some schools seem to prefer the well-rounded student. And, the well-rounded student is likelier to be happy at one of these schools.

The overall message is pretty clear. Just be you. Any student who is naturally pointy should stop trying to stuff him or herself into a mold. Don't do activities just to "look good" or try to be someone you are not. Do the things you love, do them as well as you can, and find a school that will appreciate you.

For a student who is naturally well-rounded, it would likewise be very difficult to suddenly drop many activities and just focus on one thing. This student should know it may be harder to stand out in the applicant pool, but there are schools that prefer this type of student, particularly if you do shine in one or more areas.

# SECTION 2 GETTING READY

## CHAPTER 3
## TIMELINE FOR COLLEGE PREPARATION:
## WHAT SHOULD HAPPEN WHEN
## DURING HIGH SCHOOL?

After talking with a couple friends who haven't yet started the college search process with their kids—but will, soon—I realized that creating a timeline of what to do and when to begin preparing would be helpful. So here's a fairly detailed timetable, with information gleaned from poring over countless books and websites, attending many webinars, and my own experience going through the college search process with my son. Much of this is common sense, and "working backwards."

### PRESCHOOL:

Ha ha! No, way too early. Relax.

### MIDDLE SCHOOL:

This is a good time to help make sure your child is developing organizational skills. Can he remember to do his homework and also hand it in? If not, it's a good time to help him get better. Grades don't count now (unless your child is taking an advanced class)—but they will starting in 9th grade, and it's a shame if the reason for poor grades is incomplete work rather than the student truly struggling with the difficulty of the material.

This is also a good time to pay attention to your child's interests, both academically and outside of school, and general strengths and weaknesses. These will be helpful in making an overall plan for high school.

## BEFORE HIGH SCHOOL: WHY HAVE A GENERAL PLAN BEFORE HIGH SCHOOL?

Think of the college application as a cohesive portfolio that will represent who your child is and what he or she has done during high school. A little planning will make this process easier, and will hopefully make the high school years less stressful overall!

The college application contains several sections that carry different amounts of importance. Each school will give the different sections different weight, but it is important to note that each information session we attended* for competitive schools stressed that they view the application "holistically," that is, they don't just focus on grades and test scores. They care a lot about extracurriculars, letters of recommendation, and essays. The percentages below are guidelines only, taken from a webinar I attended given by www.thecollegevine.com:
- Grades/classes taken and SAT or ACT scores (30%)
- Extra-curricular activities (25%)
- Essays (25%)
- Recommendations (15%)
- Interviews (5%)

Of the five on the list, two of them can be given consideration prior to and throughout high school:

### Grades/Classes
Students usually pick their classes for 9th grade at the end of the 8th grade year. This is a good time to look at the course catalog for your child's high school, and see what classes are offered and which are required. Are they one semester long, a whole year, or some of both? If there are courses of varying lengths, how will that affect the schedule? How much room in the schedule is there for electives over the course of four years? Guidance counselors will help with this process, but remember that most of those working in public schools have hundreds of students. If they don't know yours well, they may suggest a more generic list of classes rather than one that really suits your child. Does your child want to be able to take a particular AP Literature or math class eventually? If so, what is the path there? Don't assume it will fall into place. If our district is at all typical, or if your child's goals are at all atypical, fitting in wanted classes over four years

may not be straightforward. Now is a good time for your child to think about which subjects she likes the most and is strongest in, because it will make sense to plan to take these classes at the highest level available.

### Extracurriculars

How passionate is your child? That's what colleges want to know. A general involvement in an activity from year to year is fine, but having built upon that activity is much better. Chances are your child already has some strong interests, for example a sport or a musical instrument. Does your child plan to continue these activities in high school? Is it possible to expand upon these activities? For example, if your child plays an instrument, can he join a band or orchestra in high school, or does he just want to continue to quietly take lessons and play at home? Does your child plan to just participate in a sport, or will there be opportunities to lead as a captain, attain a personal best, referee or coach younger kids, etc.? If it looks as though he will just be a participant in his activity, then it would also be good to think about exploring other areas of interest and adding an activity or two that could give the student a chance to show leadership or excel.

It's helpful to think of high school as an experience that builds each year. For example, if a kid loves math you want to show that she chose to take as many math classes as possible each year, and progressed as far as she could. Perhaps the child can also participate in math competitions or volunteer as a math tutor. It can also mean that a child continued an extracurricular activity over three or four years of high school, and expanded his or her involvement each year by taking on more responsibility or leadership. Selective colleges are looking to see that kids are taking the most challenging classes available, developing passions, and really getting involved in activities they love. With that in mind:

### 9TH GRADE

If you've given a little thought to preparing for college already, this year will reflect that. Hopefully your child's school schedule contains not only required classes, but also classes that reflect your child's interests or that may be prerequisites for classes he or she eventually wants to take. For extracurricular activities, your child may continue a sport or other activity that he or she already likes, but it's also a great idea to try out new activities this year. There are many more clubs available at the high school level.

### 10TH GRADE

Once again, the class schedule should contain not only required classes, but also classes that reflect the student's interests and build on last year's selections. For extracurricular activities, is there a continuation of last year's activities? Is it possible to build on any? For example, can the student enter a contest or take a leadership position? If your child hasn't yet found a passion, encourage him or her to try a new club or activity, or better yet, start a new club or organization that revolves around something she cares about!

**Begin College Search.** I think this is a great year to ease into the process. This way, you will avoid feeling rushed and overwhelmed later. Good ways to begin:

Visit some nearby colleges. Look at a variety of small and large, urban and rural. Find some with different student bodies and areas of focus. Take a virtual campus tour through the college website if it is offered. This way your student can begin to get a feel for different schools and think about environments that would be a good fit.

Buy a college guide or two. See the resources section at the end of the book for suggestions. The *Fiske Guide to Colleges* (Fiske, 2018) and *The Princeton Review Guide to Colleges* (Franek, O'Toole and Soto 2017) are good places to begin.

Start talking with your child about what he or she might want in a college one day. Give some thought to his or her strengths and weaknesses, interests and preferences. Talk with friends who have older kids about their college search process. Do their kids have similar interests to yours? If so, can they suggest colleges to consider?

**Take the PSAT.** It's great practice for the SAT, and may signal areas where your child needs improvement. It will give your child an idea of how he or she will score on the SAT. This will help in the college search process by giving you an idea of which schools your student will likely be able to gain admission to based on the test scores. The PSAT offered in 10th grade is just a practice for the official PSAT offered in 11th grade, from which merit scholarship finalists are determined. I highly recommend preparing for the PSAT by taking practice tests that are available through the College Board. It is very helpful to be familiar with the types of questions and pacing of the test.

Meet with the guidance counselor. Since guidance counselors have so many students, it can be hard for them to get to know your child. However, students will need a letter of recommendation from their counselor for the college application. It's a good idea for your student to begin meeting with her guidance counselor periodically to discuss classes, goals, and interests, so the counselor can get to know her and write something other than a generic letter.

## 11TH GRADE

Hopefully by this point, because of your advance thought and planning, your child has built upon some interests and themes during his or her high school experience. 11th grade is the big year for your student to highlight what he has done for college applications. Most of what students do in 12th grade will happen after applications have been submitted.

### Classes

If your child wants to attend a more selective college, this is the year he will be taking AP or other higher-level classes, such as IB, if he didn't already take some in 10th grade. Plan ahead for next year. Are there more AP classes in preferred subject areas your student can take? If not, are there other options such as dual enrollment with a community college or online classes? Be creative. Selective colleges really want to see that kids have exhausted the resources available to them, so talk with your school and find out how your child can get the classes he or she wants in preferred subject areas next year.

### Extracurriculars

For extracurricular activities, 11th grade should reflect dedication and growth in an activity or two. It's not about quantity—it's about quality. If it hasn't happened yet, it's time for your child to roll up her sleeves and go the extra mile with one of her activities. The idea is to find opportunities for leadership and initiative and accomplishment, not just show up and warm a seat. A couple focused extracurriculars are much better than many seat-warming activities, although it's okay to have couple of those, too.

### College Search

This is the year of the college search! If you haven't already, buy some guides and start visiting colleges. Check out their web sites and do virtual tours instead of visiting the campus if they're too far away. If your child has a major in mind, check out those departments on the college websites. If not, look for schools that offer excellent general educations. Refer to some other chapters to assist with the college selection process: Chapter 7, "Clusters—Choosing Schools By Type;" Chapter 15, "What Are Selective Schools Looking For?;" Chapter 8, "Hidden Gems;" Chapter 9, "Love Your Safeties!;" Chapter 12, "How Much is School Going to Cost?;" and Chapter 1, "Each Student is a Puzzle Piece."

By the end of this school year, your child will ideally have a good list of schools that he or she wants to apply to. A good list will contain: schools that are reaches, targets, and safeties for your student; schools you know will be affordable; and only schools your child will be happy attending.

### Set Up a Spreadsheet, or Two

Help your child create a spreadsheet to organize all the information you have been collecting. My son had two, one with a list of 'colleges being considered, and one with a list of his activities during high school, including the summers. Keeping track of these things will make your life much easier! You can refer to Chapter 14, "Make a Spreadsheet, or Two!" for ideas.

### Testing

Sign up for the SAT/ACT and SAT subject tests. Take practice tests to prepare for the SAT or ACT, and possibly sign up for extra help if needed. There are free practice tests available through The College Board. Khan Academy offers free online test prep, and there are many paid services as well. Plan ahead to see when the SAT subject tests that your student wants to take are available, and make sure he or she has time to prepare beforehand.

### Recommendation Letters

In the spring of 11th grade, your student should ask a couple teachers from this year, and her guidance counselor, to write recommendation letters for college applications. Don't wait until fall of 12th grade because many teachers will have been inundated with requests by then and won't be able to take on more students.

## 12TH GRADE

With luck, and careful planning, at this point your student know where he or she will be applying to college and knows when all the applications are due!

### Classes

The classes taken in 12th grade should show that your child is continuing to challenge herself as much as possible in subject interest areas.

### Extracurriculars

Your child's extracurriculars should continue to highlight your child's passions and show that he or she has displayed some accomplishment and/or leadership in these areas.

### Testing

Have your student sign up for the SAT/ACT and/or SAT Subject tests that haven't been completed yet.

I hope this timeline is helpful, and I also hope it will come as a bit of a relief. Your student really should not spend high school totally stressed out about taking too many hard classes and jumping through hoops and participating in activities that "will look good." This can lead to burnout, and will not provide opportunities for your student to grow as a person. But if your child takes time to focus on her strengths and interests, she can take classes and pursue activities accordingly. This will not only make her happier and allow her to be the person she is meant to be, but will also do much more to impress colleges than the burned-out automaton will.

*College sessions we attended that stressed "holistic" review of application are: University of Chicago, Carnegie Mellon, University of Rochester, Swarthmore, Grinnell, Oberlin, William and Mary, MIT, and Cornell University.

# CHAPTER 4
# WHAT ABOUT THOSE SUMMERS?

Many people wonder what students should do in the summers during high school. Every information session we've attended and all the advice given by the guidebooks suggest that there is no real benefit to signing up for expensive programs at prestigious schools. It's not a bad thing—if you can afford them and your student wants to go—great! But it's more appealing to colleges if they apply (and get in) to free or low cost programs where they have to be accepted. If that doesn't work out, volunteering in an area of interest, a summer job, or internship are all good ways to spend a summer and these activities also look good to colleges. Another good way to spend time in the summer is to work on a meaningful project, since summer provides the time that most students don't have during the year. Build something, make something, write something, or compose something. If it further displays your child's interests and talents, that's a good thing! Colleges are very interested in how kids spend their summers.

# CHAPTER 5
# DON'T MAKE/LET KIDS DO ALL THE RESEARCH

When discussing the college search with parents of other high school students, it's not uncommon to hear things like, "I told my son (or daughter) that it's his college experience so it's up to him to find schools he's interested in and be on the ball about applying."

There are several problems with making, or letting, your son or daughter navigate the college search and application process on his or her own.

The first problem is that if a grown adult, whether or not she went to college, finds the process bewildering and overwhelming, then imagine how the teenager feels. Teenagers don't start out knowing anything about college, except that it's a place some people go to get more education after high school. They don't usually have the benefit of knowing many college graduates who can share their experiences, and they probably don't know much about many schools other than their superficial reputations.

Another big problem is that kids won't know to pay attention to cost, or how to assess what the cost of a particular school might be to the family. This is because kids won't be able to figure out the expected family contribution (EFC) or try the net price calculators for different schools without previous tax returns and a strong knowledge of the family's financial situation. Students might not even consider cost, wrongly assuming all colleges cost the same. Students might not know how to figure out which schools are more likely to give financial aid. Going to college is a big investment. If you wouldn't let your child take on the project of buying the next family home, you don't want him or her completely driving the college search process either.

Aside from financial considerations, your teenager may prioritize things you rather they wouldn't when looking for a school, such as the party scene or the weather. Or they may choose a school based on the reputation of the graduate programs, not the undergraduate experience, which could lead to frustration and disappointment later.

Finally, many students may not accurately assess their ability to get into certain schools. Some teenagers come up with very unrealistic lists of schools that don't have a variety of reach, target and safety schools. I know a student who was rejected by 12 of the 13 schools she applied to. That caused her and her family a lot of grief, but the situation could have been avoided if she had more schools on her list that were a better and more realistic fit for her.

The goal for every student and family should be to create a list of schools that are a good fit for the student, that contain realistic reach, target and safety schools, and that contains schools that are likely to be affordable. This goal is best achieved by including your child in the process and encouraging them to do research, but with your guidance.

# CHAPTER 6

## KIDS FEEDING THE FIRE WITH MISINFORMATION

High school is a stressful time for kids. They have to juggle their schoolwork with extracurricular activities, worry about grades, and start thinking about where they want to go to college. Many students are sleep deprived due to late nights studying and early mornings getting up for school. On top of all that, there is a lot of misinformation passed around about the college admissions process. It's so frustrating that this big, expensive event in a young person's life seems so mysterious and opaque. I'm going to list below some of the things that kids (and some adults) tell each other that are definitely NOT true.

**Myth #1** You have to do "all the right" extracurriculars to get into college.

There aren't "right" extracurricular activities to do. If there were, every application would look the same because all students would be doing exactly the same things. Colleges want to have passionate individuals attend, not robotic clones. So, if a student thinks she should join debate team because it will look good, but she doesn't really want to do it, it's probably not a good idea because she probably won't put much effort into it and there will be less time to pursue something she would really like to do. Don't think colleges will be impressed by a few half-hearted memberships in unrelated activities. Don't take my word for it, here are quotes from the websites of some of the most selective schools themselves:

Stanford University Admissions:
"Learning about your extracurricular activities and nonacademic interests helps us to discover your potential contributions to the Stanford community. Students often assume our primary concern is the number of activities in which one participates. In fact, an exceptional depth of experience in one or two activities may demonstrate your passion more than minimal participation in five or six clubs. We want to see the impact you have had on that club, in your school, or in the larger community, and we want to learn of the impact that experience has had on you."

Tufts University Admissons:
"Extracurricular Activities: In addition to evaluating an academic fit, the admissions committee looks for ways a student may contribute to the community as a whole. They will assess the level and type of involvement in each activity and may ask questions such as: Has the student been a significant contributor or leader? How has the involvement contributed to the school or larger community? Does the student have a special talent in a particular area? We do not expect all students to be team captains, class presidents, or editors-in-chief; rather, we look for meaningful involvement in their school and/or community. The Common Application allows students to list up to ten different activities, but you don't need to fill every space. Some of the most successful applicants are heavily engaged in just a few activities. Keep in mind that the Common Application is your one chance to show your extracurricular engagements: we are not able to accept a supplemental resume of activities."

Princeton University Admissions FAQ:
"We review each application individually to get a sense of that student's particular combination of strengths. We don't have a profile of the ideal applicant or the ideal class. In fact, one of Princeton's greatest strengths is the variety of talents, personal qualities, experiences and points of view in each incoming class. There are some qualities we hope all Princeton students share: integrity, a deep interest in learning and a devotion to both

academic and non-academic pursuits. Many students also bring distinctive academic and extracurricular talents and achievements. Beyond those fundamental qualities, we consider how each candidate might contribute to the community we will bring together for that year's class."

**Myth #2** You need to play an organized sport or colleges won't be interested in you.

There are certainly very sports-focused colleges that actively recruit athletes, but that is definitely not the sole focus for many schools, including many of the most competitive schools. That's not to say a school wouldn't love to have an accomplished athlete, but schools are looking for students with other talents too. If a student is a below average athlete who doesn't really enjoy sports, it would be a waste of time to spend all the time that is required to play a school and/or club sport when he could be spending that time pursuing something he is really passionate about. The same information applies here about "doing the right extracurriculars." Most colleges are looking to fill out their student bodies with kids who will be successful in many different areas and who bring diverse talents to the school.

**Myth #3** You should join as many honor societies as possible because they look good.

This is almost the same myth as joining "all the right" extracurriculars. Honor societies can provide opportunities for leadership and deeper levels of service and commitment, but just joining one will do little to impress most colleges. In some schools, more than half the members of each class are members of honor societies, so just being a member will hardly make you stand out.

A blogger from Ohio State University wrote in her post "*Why You should, (and Should Not) Join an Honors Society*" (Xu, 2014), "Like all other organizations, make your involvement meaningful. Don't join honors societies just because they are 'honors.' Even if you join a bunch of societies, you won't have anything to show for them in the end if you don't make your enrollment worthwhile. Do some careful research beforehand, and make sure that a society is reputable, active, and beneficial to your specific academic and professional needs."

A blog post on theivycoach.com (2012) website states (perhaps a little harshly): "The fact is that being in the National Honor Society does as little for you in highly selective college admissions as tying your shoelaces with bunny ears as compared to the other more advanced shoelace tying process. And why is it so meaningless? Because almost every student who applies for admission to Princeton, Dartmouth, Harvard, Yale, Cornell, Penn, Columbia, and Brown are members of their high school's National Honor Society. College admissions officers at highly selective colleges look for ways to distinguish applicants. What they don't look for are ways the applicants are all the same. That would be a waste! So don't get so excited about being in the National Honor Society. Colleges don't care about meaningless honors. They care about passion, intellectual curiosity, perseverance, determination, hard work, and talent."

But even if you're not looking for admission to an Ivy League or similar school, Jennifer Ziegenfus, A Towson University advisor, who was interviewed by the The Lance (DuBro, 2015), the Linganore High School news website, stated that Towson Admissions much prefers extracurricular quality to quantity. "Towson University would rather a student excel in their activities than simply add an activity to a resume to fill space."

**Myth #4** Gaining Admission To the Most Selective Schools Is Random Chance Once You Have Good Grades and Test Scores

I've already referred to this article, *"How to Get Into Harvard and the Ivy League, by a Harvard Alum,"* (Cheng, Allen, 2018) and the author, in addition to being admitted to Harvard, was also accepted at Princeton, MIT, and Stanford and all the other schools he applied to. His argument is that there are certain students who will gain admission anywhere they apply because they truly stand out, and there is a gray area of students who have strong GPAs and test scores but a rather unremarkable record on extracurriculars who might gain admission here and there at a highly competitive school, but who can't count on it. He is blunt (his word) and to the point, but what he says has been corroborated by information sessions we've attended at places like University of Chicago and Swarthmore. Even for kids who don't care to gain admission to the most selective schools, it's good to understand this fundamental concept because the same ideas apply to all schools (see previous quote from Towson University representative).

The article is long, so I will attempt to summarize the overall concept here. We know that top schools want top students. These students will bring talent and drive with them that will make success in college and in life very likely. This will ultimately be great for the school because successful students who go on to have distinguished careers make the school look good!

So, how do these schools determine who will be the most successful students who are most likely to go on to have the most successful accomplishments later in life? The schools look to past accomplishments. High GPA (in challenging classes) and high test scores are a good starting point. But then they look at the rest of the application. They want to see a record of accomplishment in extracurricular activities as well. This goes back to not joining a bunch of clubs just because they "look good" and then just warming a seat. This is about finding a passion or talent and taking it to the highest level possible. This is where colleges look for leaders, those that have won competitions, those that have worked hard to achieve goals, and students who have found other ways of rising above the crowd in their area of interest. Cheng calls this distinguished area of accomplishment a "spike."

Once the college is satisfied that this strong student with great test scores has also distinguished herself in some way, they look to other parts of the application. How about those recommendations? At more than one information session we attended, the college representative emphasized the need to find teachers that will give you a positive recommendation. Of course everyone in the audience laughed to hear that. But clearly, some kids are sending in applications with recommendations that are negative, or only neutral. An example given at an information session at Grinnell College was, "this student can work well with other students if he regards them as his intellectual equal." That was a red flag for Grinnell. Teachers can also rate how the student compares to other students, so obviously, if a teacher says this is one of the best students she has ever taught, that sounds much better than saying that a student is average. For a really well written and hilarious parody of a negative recommendation, see this *"Letter of Recommendation for a Basic Male MFA Applicant"* (Brewer, Emma, 2018) from McSweeney's.

Finally, every information session we've attended emphasized the importance of the essay. You can refer to Chapter 17, "How to Craft the College Admissions Essay," for more detail, but in brief, all schools seem to make a similar point which is that they want authenticity. They want the essay to highlight the student's passions and let them get to know the student in a way they can't from the rest of the application. They don't want the student to write what she thinks the school wants to hear. Another funny point brought up in several information sessions is that they don't want students to overuse the thesaurus and put too many difficult, clunky words in the essay that the reader needs to look up. So, if your student's essay has the word "perspicacious" in it, it might be worth seeing if there is another word that can get the point across.

**Myth #5** If a college is undecided about you, they will go all the way back to your grades from 6th grade to decide if they will accept you.

This gem was brought home to me by my middle schooler, although I'm not really sure if anyone in high school believes this or not. Middle school grades do not appear on high school transcripts, except that in some districts, students who take high school classes in middle school, for example geometry or a foreign language, will have just those grades appear on their transcripts. This does not seem to be true everywhere, so you should check with your local school system to see if these specific grades will appear on the transcript.

# SECTION 3 CHOOSING SCHOOLS

## CHAPTER 7 CLUSTERS—CHOOSING COLLEGE BY TYPE

I'm often surprised when I hear about kids who apply to schools that seem really different from one another, for example, an international research university with 30,000 undergraduates and a small, regional liberal arts college. When I ask what qualities the different schools have that make them attractive to the student, the answer is often more about geographic location or name recognition than it is about what the school actually has to offer, so I thought I would write about a process that we have found helpful in generating a list of schools of interest—creating "clusters." Clusters of schools are schools that all have the qualities that are important to your student. It's possible that two different students will have some, but not all, the same schools on their lists because they are using a slightly different set of criteria when creating their clusters.

This method is great for generating a cohesive list of schools that have the qualities that are important for your child. If done well, it has the added benefit of including reach, target, and safety schools, because instead of using prestige or selectivity as a factor for adding a school to the list, the student is looking for courses of study, particular opportunities, type of students, or some other quality that she finds important, and these qualities can usually be found at schools with different selectivity levels. This process is also a lot of fun because you might end up learning about schools you've never heard of before—but that may be a great fit for your student. After all, finding a school that is a good fit is the most important part!

The first step to finding a "cluster" of schools is to figure out what qualities are important to your child. Start with a list that includes things your child cares about in a school such as:
•Size
•Strongest academic departments
•Undergraduate research or study abroad opportunities
•Type of social life
•Type of students
•Sports and club opportunities
•Location
•Accessibility of professors

There are so many different factors to consider, and they won't all be equally important for each student, so it's important to figure out your student's individual priorities. For example, my son likes hearing about campuses that are also arboretums; obviously this particular quality won't matter to a lot of students.

Once you have a list of qualities that are important to your student, you can try to find some schools that have these qualities by looking at college guides, talking with friends, doing some research online, or visiting campuses that are close by. It can be difficult to find a school or two that seem like good fits, but once you do, it's easier to find some similar schools to add to your cluster. A helpful next step is looking at your college guides for suggestions. In the *Fiske Guide to Colleges* (Fiske, 2017) for example, at the end of each school entry is a section called "overlaps," where you can see other schools kids typically apply to when they apply to the school you're reading about. Similarly, in *The Princeton Review Guide to Colleges* (Franek, O'Toole and Soto 2017), there is a section, "Applicants Also Look At" with three categories: "...and Often Prefer," "...And Sometimes Prefer," and "...Rarely Prefer."

These are terrific starting points. Often the schools listed in these sections share similar important qualities.

For example, if you consider Rensselaer Polytechnic Institute, the "overlaps" in the *Fiske Guide to Colleges* (Fiske, 2017) are: Carnegie Mellon, Cornell University, Georgia Tech, MIT, and Worcester Polytechnic. These makes sense as they are all either tech schools or offer very strong engineering programs. They have similar numbers of undergraduates: Rensselaer, 5,778; Carnegie Mellon, 6,500; MIT, 4,489; and Worcester Polytechnic, 4,085; the exceptions are Cornell, 14,471; and Georgia Tech, 13,572.

Lists from *The Princeton Review Guide to Colleges* (Franek, O'Toole and Soto 2017) are similar with students often preferring MIT and Cornell, sometimes preferring Boston University (16,082 undergrads), Carnegie Mellon, and University of Rochester (6,000 undergrads); and rarely preferring SUNY Binghamton (13,045 undergrads), Rochester Institute of Technology (12,186 undergrads), Syracuse University (14,127 undergrads), Clarkson University (3,147 undergrads), and Worcester Polytechnic. For a kid interested in a tech school or strong engineering program, this list of schools is a good starting point. Of course, there are many good tech and engineering schools that aren't mentioned here, but if you look at some of the schools that came up as an overlap for Rensselaer and look at their lists of overlapping schools, the list will really start to take shape. From there you can see what other qualities the schools do or don't share that are important to your child, and add or subtract schools from the list accordingly. As I mentioned before, these schools also have a range of selectivity. Rensselaer accepts 44% of applicants, MIT accepts 8%, and Rochester Institutes of Technology accepts 55%. If your student finds the qualities he wants in all these schools, he may also (depending on the strength of his application) have found a reach, target, and safety school.

One potential problem with this method is that sometimes the overlaps seem to be a list of schools that have similar prestige, but don't necessarily have other similarities. This seems to mainly be a problem for Ivy League Schools (and those with Ivy League reputations). For example, Princeton's overlap schools are: Harvard, Yale, Stanford, and MIT. And University of Pennsylvania's overlaps are Brown, Columbia, Cornell, Harvard, Stanford, and Yale. No surprises here, but it's interesting to note that in the *Fiske Guide*'s opening paragraph about the University of Pennsylvania it states that it is more similar to Georgetown and Northwestern. For a kid who likes the University of Pennsylvania, Georgetown and Northwestern might be better schools to add to the cluster than the other Ivy League or Ivy-type schools listed in the overlap section.

Once you find schools that are truly similar because they have the qualities you are looking for as opposed to similar name recognition or prestige, the search becomes a lot more interesting.

# CHAPTER 8

# HIDDEN GEMS

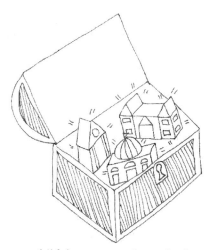

Once you and your child have gone through the process of finding a "cluster" of schools with similar qualities, you will hopefully have created a list that contains reaches, targets, and safeties. It's fun to learn about schools that have similar strengths, philosophies, and environments. Through this process you can discover amazing schools that seem to offer very specific opportunities for the students who want them, and they may not be schools that you have necessarily heard of before.

A little effort can set you off on a path of discovery that may lead to a happier student in the long run. For example, since my son is interested in studying physics in college, we started looking at some of the obvious technical schools, although not very large universities, since he finds them overwhelming. After doing a bit more research, we found that in addition to technical universities there are many small liberal arts colleges (LACs) that have strong physics departments. We were familiar with many of these LACs, such as Williams, Reed, Grinnell, Swarthmore, and Carleton College. The idea of attending a LAC for college can be very appealing because of the personalized attention a student can receive. And, sometimes, LACs offer greater opportunities for undergraduate research. For a kid who might get lost in a big university, this could be a great environment. In addition to the schools we were familiar with, through our research we discovered a math and science focused LAC (the only one of its kind) called Harvey Mudd College. Although it's well known in science and academic circles, it was new to us.

We were thrilled to know about so many strong LACs for physics, but one drawback is that all of the LACs I mentioned are highly selective. We wanted to find a great LAC for physics that could also be a safety school. Then we came across charts of the schools that send the most students to graduate programs (these came from the Reed College website). I also added a 4th image that was the old version of these charts, because both the new (Tables 8.1 and 8.2) and old (Tables 8.3 and 8.4) charts contain lesser-known schools in the physics column:

Table 8.1

## Undergraduate Origins of Doctoral Degrees

Percentage ranking of doctorates, by academic field, conferred upon graduates of listed institutions.

| Rank | All Disciplines | Science and Math | Social Sciences | Humanities and Arts |
|------|-----------------|------------------|-----------------|---------------------|
| 1 | Calif. Inst. of Tech. | Calif. Inst. of Tech. | Swarthmore | New England Conserv. of Music |
| 2 | Harvey Mudd | Harvey Mudd | Bard College at Simon's Rock | St. John's, MD |
| 3 | Swarthmore | Carleton | **Reed** | Swarthmore |
| 4 | **Reed** | MIT | Haverford | **Reed** |
| 5 | Carleton | **Reed** | Carleton | Oberlin |
| 6 | MIT | Swarthmore | Pomona | Juilliard |
| 7 | Grinnell | Haverford | Amherst | Cleveland Inst. of Music |
| 8 | Haverford | Univ. of Chicago | Williams | Yale |
| 9 | Princeton | Grinnell | Harvard | St. John's, NM |
| 10 | Harvard | Pomona | Bryn Mawr | Amherst |

Table 8.2

## Percentage Ranking by Specific Fields of Study

| Rank | Life Sciences | Physical Sciences | Psychology | Other Social Sciences* | Humanities |
|------|---------------|-------------------|------------|------------------------|------------|
| 1 | Calif. Inst. of Tech. | Calif. Inst. of Tech. | Univ. Puerto Rico - Aguadilla | Swarthmore | St. John's, MD |
| 2 | **Reed** | Harvey Mudd | **Reed** | Bard College at Simon's Rock | **Reed** |
| 3 | Swarthmore | **Reed** | Wellesley | **Reed** | Swarthmore |
| 4 | Carleton | NM Institute Mining/Tech. | Vassar | Harvard | St. John's, NM |
| 5 | Grinnell | MIT | Haverford | Univ. of Chicago | Amherst |
| 6 | MIT | Carleton | Barnard | Carlton | Carleton |
| 7 | Haverford | Swarthmore | Williams | Williams | Bryn Mawr |
| 8 | Harvey Mudd | Haverford | Pomona | Amherst | Yale |
| 9 | Pomona | Wabash | Bard College at Simon's Rock | Pomona | Harvard |
| 10 | Univ. of Chicago | Grinnell | Grinnell | Bryn Mawr | Bard |

*Does not include psychology, education, or communications and librarianship.

Table 8.3

## Undergraduate Origins of Doctoral Degrees

Percentage ranking of doctorates, all disciplines, conferred upon graduates of listed institutions.

| 1975-2004 | 1995-2004 | 1997-2006 | 2003-2012 |
|-----------|-----------|-----------|-----------|
| Calif. Inst. of Tech. | Calif. Inst. of Tech. | Calif. Inst. of Tech. | Calif. Inst. of Tech. |
| Harvey Mudd | Harvey Mudd | Harvey Mudd | Harvey Mudd |
| **Reed** | Swarthmore | **Reed** | Swarthmore |
| Swarthmore | **Reed** | Swarthmore | **Reed** |
| MIT | MIT | MIT | Carleton |
| Univ. of Chicago | Carleton | Carleton | MIT |
| Carleton | Oberlin | Grinnell | Grinnell |
| Oberlin | Bryn Mawr | Bryn Mawr | Harvard |
| Bryn Mawr | Univ. of Chicago | Univ. of Chicago | Princeton |
| Pomona | Grinnell | Oberlin | Univ. of Chicago |

Source: National Science Foundation and Integrated Postsecondary Education Data System.

Table 8.4

| Rank | Physics | Social Sciences | English & Literature | Humanities |
|---|---|---|---|---|
| 1 | Calif. Inst. of Tech. | Swarthmore | Simon's Rock of Bard | California State System |
| 2 | Harvey Mudd | Bryn Mawr | St. John's College | Thomas |
| 3 | MIT | Grinnell | Amherst | Mt. Aloysius |
| 4 | **Reed** | **Reed** | Yale | Univ. of NH Manchester |
| 5 | Univ. of Chicago | Univ. of Chicago | **Reed** | Univ. of Puerto Rico Aguadilla |
| 6 | Rice | Harvard | Swarthmore | St. John's |
| 7 | Carleton | Pomona | Bryn Mawr | **Reed** |
| 8 | Princeton | Wesleyan | Wesleyan | Amherst |
| 9 | Harvard | Oberlin | Williams | Bryn Mawr |
| 10 | Lawrence | Macalester | Oberlin | Yale |

On the old chart, the surprise school for me was Lawrence University, in Appleton, WI. I'd never heard of it before and it was really cool to see it among all these better-known schools. I'm disappointed that it's not on the most recent chart, but it could mean that it just fell down a few places, which would still make it a good choice for a student hoping to earn a PhD in physics one day. Although Lawrence University is not on the most recent list, Wabash College is on the newer chart in the physical sciences category.

Both Lawrence University and Wabash College have acceptance rates of 63%, so they could be great "target" or "safety" school for many students who want to study physics and go to graduate school one day, but who might not be able to get into Harvard or MIT (which is most students). And, as a bonus, both schools offer generous merit aid according to their websites. This is true for many lesser-known LACs. For a top student who wants to go on to earn a PhD in physics one day, Lawrence University or Wabash College could end up being a more economical way to achieve that goal.

The idea of hidden gem colleges is not new, but it's a fun quest when looking at colleges to try to find one that has the specific qualities you are looking for. There is a terrific book by Loren Pope that can help you find some great schools you might not be familiar with: *Colleges That Change Lives: 40 Schools That Will Change the Way You Think About College* (Pope, 2012). Good luck finding your hidden gems!

# CHAPTER 9

# LOVE YOUR SAFETIES

As I obsessively poked around online forums and blogs reading about the college search experience for high school students, I was saddened by the number of kids who are crushed by not getting into the schools on their lists. Again and again, many kids apply only to highly selective schools (which are reaches for just about everyone), and then they throw in a "safety" as an afterthought. Often the safety bears no resemblance to the other schools on the list and it's clear that other than knowing she could get in, the student spent almost no time learning about the school and whether it would be a good "fit."

This heartbreak is completely avoidable with some planning. All students should apply to safety schools that they can love! It's important to have realistic expectations about what are reach, target, and safety schools for your student and spend as much time researching safety schools as the more selective schools. Ideally your child will be excited about the opportunities and environments at every school she applies to.

A good way to get started is to figure out what constitutes a reach school, target school, and safety school for your student. The *Fiske Guide to Colleges* (Fiske, 2018) and *The Princeton Review Guide to Colleges* (Franek, O'Toole and Soto 2017) are great places to get started because you can learn what SAT/ACT scores the middle 50% of accepted students have at each school, as well as their GPA and class rank. It's also important to look at the percentage of admitted students. Another really important point to note is that for the most selective schools, where 25% or fewer students are accepted, just having a GPA or SAT score in the range does not make it a target school—they should still go in the reach category. Why is this? According to the folks at www.collegevine.com and Allen Cheng at www.prepscholar.com, the most selective schools receive many applications from students with excellent GPAs and test scores, so they are looking for more than good numbers. You can read more about this in Chapter 15, "What Are Selective Schools Looking For?" However, less selective schools will often admit students who meet certain GPA and test score results.

Once the student has a handle on what her scores and other qualifications might mean in terms of acceptance into various types of schools, hopefully she will assess what she wants to find at any of those colleges—safety or reach—once she gets there. Is she looking for a great music program or a strong history department? Study abroad? Does she want access to internships or research opportunities? A lot of school spirit where everyone cheers on the sports teams on weekends? Whatever the qualities are, make sure that all the schools on the list have them and that your student feels like she could be happy at all the places she applies to.

# CHAPTER 10

# NAME BRAND-ITIS, AND WHAT EVERYONE SHOULD KNOW ABOUT COLLEGE RANKINGS

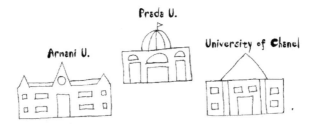

I've started, stopped, and restarted writing this chapter because it's not a straightforward one to write. It's difficult because it is nearly impossible to find consistent data in meaningful categories that can help determine what schools are the "best." There are also so many possible categories one can look at to determine "best." However, I did my best to tackle a few categories.

I think everyone would agree that there are certain elite schools that people tend to view with more awe and admiration than others. Many students (and their parents) yearn to gain admission to schools in the Ivy League and a handful of others, such as Stanford, MIT, and liberal arts colleges such as Amherst and Swarthmore. But why?

One place many people turn to is the U.S. News and World Report for college rankings. For many, this is the final word on whether a school is good or not. Therefore, I think this insightful and rather scathing article, *"15 Things to Know About U.S. News' College Rankings"* (O'Shaughnessy, Lynn), is a must-read for everyone. I recommend her site in general, and her overall message is to not go into crazy debt sending kids to college when there are so many colleges out there where your kid can get a fantastic education and a good deal, if you're willing to look outside of the "top 100 list" on U.S. News and World Report. In the article, she debunks the myth that there is any value in these college "rankings" at all because the methods used to rank schools are deeply flawed and often gamed. And college tuitions are often tightly linked to their number in the ranking—the higher the ranking, the more expensive the school. However, she writes, "One of the perverse aspects about the rankings is that turning out thoughtful, articulate young men and women, who can write cogently and think critically won't budge a school's ranking up even one spot. U.S. News and World Report doesn't even attempt to measure the type of learning going on at schools."

I will add that although I agree with most of what she says in her article, I disagree with her disdain for merit aid. Many schools offer need-blind admission and many offer a lot of need-based financial aid. I think it makes sense for institutions that exalt learning and the intellect to reward and lure some of the top applicants with merit aid. She herself suggests finding schools that award merit aid in another article, *"Looking for Great College Bargains"* (O'Shaughnessy, Lynn).

So, if U.S. News and World Report can't tell us which schools are the best, where else should we turn?

**The Best Professors?**

I think most people would agree that a "top school" should have excellent professors. On that note, a friend of mine from college, Steve Runge, is part of an academic couple. Together, he and his wife have attended: Colby College (undergraduate); Syracuse University, University of Wisconsin-Madison, Simmons College, (graduate); and they have been employed by: Syracuse University, University of Wisconsin-Madison, Madison Area Technical College, St. Lawrence University, Grinnell College, Northeastern University, and Boston College (whew!). On top of that, they have colleagues working at nearly 100 other colleges and universities across the country with whom they have shared their experiences.

Steve says, "The quality of professors is high. Everywhere. Don't even worry about mastery of material and teaching ability: that's going to be the same at Ivy Leagues and B schools. (The job market is so tight that highly qualified people are cobbling together careers adjuncting at four schools.) If they're depending primarily on part-time, contingent faculty, that means they're cutting into bone. I've been an adjunct, and know we do good work, but a high percent of adjuncts and part-time faculty means a really fractured intellectual environment. (In other words, I had no time to be part of students' lives outside of class)." He also made this very interesting point. "Do find out how many professors are full time/tenure-track, and how many are minorities or women, and how many minorities and women are in leadership roles. High percentages for both are a good indication about an administration still centered on teaching and doing it ethically. The job market is SO tight that if a school lags in hiring minorities and women, that's a warning signal about something wrong with the culture."

Fortunately, *The Princeton Review Guide to Colleges* (Franek, O'Toole and Soto 2017), contains two categories in each school listing called: "professors interesting" and "professors accessible." They are both on a scale from 60-99, and are based on levels of surveyed students' agreement or disagreement with the statements, "Your instructors are good teachers," and "Your instructors are accessible outside the classroom."

Here are sample responses to these categories from undergraduate students at the following schools:

**Some Really Low Ratings:**
Harvard: 65 and 62
California Institute of Technology: 68 and 69
University of California—Los Angeles: 67 and 63
University of Rhode Island: 68 and 68
University of Maryland—College Park: 66 and 62
University of Missouri: 68 and 68

**Low to Medium Ratings:**
University of Michigan—Ann Arbor: 71 and 73
Massachusetts Institute of Technology: 76 and 78
University of Virginia: 76 and 79
Texas A&M: 73 and 71
Columbia: 75 and 72
Rensselaer: 69 and 81
Princeton: 81 and 73
Carnegie Mellon: 79 and 83
Syracuse University: 74 and 71

**Higher Ratings**
Stanford: 81 and 83
Yale: 86 and 83
Amherst: 89 and 86
Allegheny College: 90 ad 86
University of Chicago: 82 and 81

**High Ratings**
Brown University: 92 and 88
DePauw University: 89 and 94
Swarthmore: 98 and 93
Bryn Mawr: 96 and 92
William and Mary: 94 and 95
Dickinson: 90 and 92
College of Wooster: 96 and 98
Whitman: 95 and 99

I picked the schools above at random, and you can do this same exercise if you have the book. Based on the above ratings by their own students, DePauw University and College of Wooster are much better schools than Harvard and Princeton, if you value how good the professors are and how accessible they are to students. Interestingly, classes at Harvard are known for not just being taught by teacher's assistants, but by fellow undergraduates (see the article, *"Harvard Undergrads Are Teaching Each Other and Harvard Doesn't Want to Talk About It,"* (Finegold, S., 2013) in the Harvard Political Review.

The Website www.niche.com is another good source to see how students at various schools rate their own professors. When I mentioned that figuring out "best" in any category is not a straightforward process, there are frustrating contradictions between the Princeton and Niche findings. For example, University of Rochester's ratings in *The Princeton Review's* categories are 73 and 71 respectively (low). However, www.niche.com's comprehensive professor ranking system shows wildly different results. In 2018 Colleges with the Best Professors in America, University of Rochester ranks at #28. California Institute of Technology, with very low scores in the Princeton Guide, earns #7 on the list! www.niche.com's rankings are "based on key statistics and student reviews using data from the U.S. Department of Education. Top-ranked colleges have diverse, accomplished, and well paid faculty members that are highly rated by students." You can see their methodology at about.niche.com/methodology/best-college-professors, which does look truly comprehensive. If a school you are interested in has very different ratings in these different resources, it would be worth doing further investigation to try to get an accurate picture of the professors at the school and the students' experience with them.

## How About Starting Salaries and Mid-Career Earnings?

This is yet another area that is not 100% straightforward because I don't think there has really been a good, comprehensive study on this topic. Many people will refer to a study published in 1999 by the researchers Alan Krueger and Stacy Berg Dale referred to in this article, "*Who Needs Harvard*" (Easterbrook, Gregg, 2004). The study found that students who attended more elite schools did indeed earn more than students who attended lesser-known schools, but Easterbrook wrote, "Krueger and Dale studied what happened to students who were accepted at an Ivy or a similar institution, but chose instead to attend a less sexy, 'moderately selective' school. It turned out that such students had, on average, the same income twenty years later as graduates of the elite colleges. Krueger and Dale found that for students bright enough to win admission to a top school, later income 'varied little, no matter which type of college they attended.' In other words, the student, not the school, was responsible for the success."

A more recent version of this study that apparently used more and better data was conducted by the same researchers and written about in the article, "*Revisiting the Value of Elite Colleges*" (Leonhardt, David, 2011). The results are similar but they also focus on SAT scores and the correlation between SAT scores and future earnings, regardless of where the student chooses to attend college, "A student with a 1,400 SAT score who went to Penn State but applied to [U] Penn earned as much, on average, as a student with a 1,400 who went to [U] Penn." One big problem with both the old and more recent study are that even the less elite colleges used to collect the data are still pretty selective (you can see the list of colleges at the end of the article). It really doesn't tell us anything about the future success of students who attend lower-tiered schools.

An Atlantic Monthly article, "*Does Going to a Selective College Matter?*" (White, Gillian, 2015), uses data collected from a study by Eric Eide and Mark Showalter of Brigham Young University and Michael Hilmer of San Diego State University. These results are slightly different from the studies cited above. The results show that attending a top tier or mid-tier school makes little difference in future earnings for most majors, such as those in engineering or the sciences. However, it did seem to matter for business majors, perhaps due to the networking opportunities that come with a prestigious school. For social science and education majors there was also an earning boost that came from attending a better-ranked school.

Also mentioned in this article, those that went on to attend graduate school (no matter what tier of undergraduate school they attended) enjoyed higher later career earnings. That would be a good argument for not worrying too much about where your child attends school to earn a bachelor's degree, and also for trying to avoid too much debt. Save the money for graduate school. Lynn O'Shaughnessy has a good article about this, *"Don't Pay $280,000 for a bachelor's degree."*

If you are curious about earnings for a particular major at a particular school, you can go to the website www.payscale.com for a comparison. Unfortunately, it is not clear how they collect their data.

One critical last point on the subject is mentioned by D. Leonhardt (2011) in *"Revisiting the Value of Elite Colleges,"* "a few major groups did not fit the pattern: black students, Latino students, low-income students and students whose parents did not graduate from college. 'For them, attending a more selective school increased earnings significantly,'" Krueger (2000) wrote in his article, *"Economic Scene; Children Smart Enough to Get Into Elite Schools May Not Need to Bother."* "'Perhaps they benefit from professional connections they would not otherwise have. Perhaps they acquire habits or skills that middle-class and affluent students have already acquired in high school or at home.'"

Since one way to boost future earnings seems to be attending graduate school, it might be worth figuring out which schools send the highest percentage of graduates on for further study.

**Colleges That Send the Most Graduates on to Graduate School?**
There are various lists and resources where you can find the colleges or universities that send the most students on to graduate school and/or to receive their PhDs. You have to be careful as the most important number is the percentage of students who go on to graduate school rather than total number, as 100 kids going to grad school from a class of 500 is very different than 200 kids going to grad school from a class of 5,000.

The following resources use different criteria such as how many go to graduate school within one year vs. eventually, or in various disciplines:

- Within one year: *"11 Colleges Where Graduates Pursue Continuing Education"* (Ross, Kelly Mae, 2018).
- Colleges with highest percentages of kids going on to graduate studies by discipline: *"The Colleges Where PhD's Get Their Start"*

(O'Shaughnessy, Lynn).

- Top Producers of Science PhDs: *"Top 50 Schools That Produce Science PhDs"* (O'Shaughnessy, Lynn, 2010).
- Top Producers of History PhDs: *"Privileging History: Trends in the Undergraduate Origins of History PhDs"* (Townsend, Robert B., 2005) (In this article, scroll down to second list which has proportion, not overall number, of students going on to earn PhDs.)

Once again, it's not crystal clear that name-brands schools offer a strong advantage if you want to attend graduate school one day. Although it's true that many of the elite name-brand schools show up on (and top) the lists, there are many schools that continue to show up that don't have the same name recognition, such as Kalamazoo, Knox, Wabash, Grinnell, and Lawrence University, among others. However, many schools don't appear on these lists. I haven't found any resources showing where students end up getting their graduate degrees, unless you go to the websites of individual colleges that post this kind of data, which is very time-consuming. I can't figure out whether applicants from Kalamazoo and Princeton with the same grades have the same chance of entering a top-notch PhD program. It does seem that although a school may not have name recognition "on the street," there are many schools that are well respected within academia and their students are readily accepted into graduate programs.

Another thing to consider...
### Where Did Fortune 500 CEOs Go to School?
Many people may assume that they're all Ivy League graduates, but CEOs of Fortune 500 companies come from all types of schools, "Overall, the Fortune 500 crew attended 220 different colleges for their undergraduate degrees," although as you can see in *"Top Ten Colleges of Fortune 500 CEOs"* (Mulhere, Kaitlyn, 2016), there are schools that produce more CEOs than others. This Forbes article, *"The Universities that Produce the Most CEO's"* (Adams, Susan, 2013), stresses that where the undergraduate was earned does matter. Interestingly, they are not all Ivy League or similar schools: Penn State and University of Miami in Ohio are among the top 10 producers of top CEOs. Here is another list (of a variety of schools) where top CEOs earned their undergraduate degrees: *"America's Top CEOs and their College Degrees"* (Williams, Terri, 2018).

So, if a student aspires to be a CEO of a Fortune 500 company, going to an Ivy League schools doesn't necessarily provide an advantage.

### In Summary

There are plenty of other categories that can be explored in the quest for "best" school. I think that if a student values great professors, high potential future earnings, potential acceptance into a graduate program, and even the chance to be a CEO of a company one day, there are many schools outside of the prestigious "name-brand" list that will provide these opportunities. It seems pretty clear that it is the intelligence, drive, and motivation (and apparently test scores) of the student who will determine future success, rather than where she ultimately chooses to go to school. That's not to say all schools are created equally, so it makes sense to find the schools that provide certain opportunities (such as high graduate school placement rates). But these schools won't all be name brand. The good news is, there are choices! And they're not all nearly impossible to get into or completely unaffordable.

The people who do seem to get the biggest boost from name brand schools are students from disadvantaged backgrounds. And this group faces another hurdle: *"These Four Charts Show How The SAT Favors Rich, Educated Families"* (Goldfarb, Zachary, 2014). If these students can overcome that hurdle, they are in luck. The name brand schools tend to be very generous with need-based aid.

For an alternate look at college rankings: Money Magazine's *"These Are the 27 Best Colleges in America"* (2018) has its own ranking using its own methodology.

A final word from my friend, Steve, "The key is that no matter where your kid goes to college, he'll learn a ton and be prepared for career and life, because that's exactly what all colleges specialize in and really do work hard at. Whit (Steve's wife) and I have worked both at top flight and b-schools, small liberal arts colleges and big urban universities. Ninety five (95%) of students at all of these places were happy, productive, and doing amazing things."

# CHAPTER 11

# MORE WAYS TO THINK ABOUT "GOOD" SCHOOLS

I read the article, *"Here's How We Ranked The Most Underrated Colleges In America,"* (Kiersz, Andy 2015), and thought I should share it here. Business Insider determined which schools are underrated by comparing their rating on U.S. News & World Report to rankings with The Payscale College Salary Report. The lowest ranked schools in the U.S. News & World Report with the highest mid-career salary earnings of its graduates determined their designation as "underrated." Of course, future salary isn't the only thing to take into account when choosing schools, but in these days of incredibly high tuitions and uncertainty about the future, it's not a bad place to start. I wish they also included a list of overrated schools, and schools whose status rankings match their earning potential rankings. The Business Insider article has a great graph, but then only offers the data on the underrated schools. I looked around quite a bit for a similarly credible measure of overrated schools, but couldn't find anything more than opinion pieces.

This is probably a good time to once again mention the excellent book, *Colleges That Change Lives: 40 Schools That Will Change the Way You Think About Colleges* (Pope, 2102). He highlights many schools, most of them lesser known, that provide wonderful opportunities for their students.

# SECTION 4 COST

# CHAPTER 12
# HOW MUCH IS COLLEGE GOING TO COST?

We all know that college is expensive. It's daunting to think about sending a son or daughter off to school and how you're going to pay for it. Ideally, we would all find the best education for our child for the best price, but how do you start?

## In-State Tuition at State School

When just looking at sticker price, the first choice for affordability will almost always be in-state tuition at your state school. There are a few exceptions to this with some schools charging out-of-state students the same tuition as in-state students, but these are uncommon. On top of the usually relatively low in-state tuition, most scholarships offered by state schools will go to their in-state students. You can access information on tuition for individual state schools in *The Princeton Review: The Best 382 Colleges* (Franek, Robert; O'Toole, Kristen; and Soto, David 2017) and on individual college websites. However, sometimes the state school options won't be the best fit for your child. What if you want to expand your options?

## Out of State Tuition at a Public School

The next category of affordability when looking at sticker price is usually out-of-state tuition for a state school. That's not always true, as out-of-state tuition for many state schools can be as high as some private school tuition (see University of California system as an example). So check those prices to find out-of-state schools that are affordable.

## Private Schools

And then there are private schools. Most of them are very expensive. According to the *Fiske Guide to Colleges* (Fiske, 2017) the range for cost of attendance is about $40,000-$68,000. Per year. This is where it gets tricky. Since these are the sticker prices, how can you figure out how much you will actually pay?

## Expected Family Contribution (EFC)

The very first place to start is to find out what your EFC is. This is a number you will learn when you fill out the Free Application for Federal Student Aid (FAFSA), but you can also use the calculator on the College Board website: bigfuture.collegeboard.org/pay-for-college/paying-your-share/expected-family-contribution-calculator.

*From the FAFSA website:* The EFC is a measure of your family's financial strength and is calculated according to a formula established by law. Your family's taxed and untaxed income, assets, and benefits (such as unemployment or Social Security) are all considered in the formula. Also considered are your family size and the number of family members who will attend college during the year.

The information you report on your Free Application for Federal Student Aid (FAFSA) or your FAFSA4caster is used to calculate your EFC. Schools use the EFC to determine your federal student aid eligibility and financial aid award.

Note: Your EFC is not the amount of money your family will have to pay for college nor is it the amount of federal student aid you will receive. It is a number used by your school to calculate the amount of federal student aid you are eligible to receive.

The EFC is a calculation used by the federal government to determine eligibility for Pell Grants and subsidized Stafford loans, but is NOT an indication of what you will actually have to pay in college tuition.

## Net Price Calculators

The next step in trying to determine the cost of attendance at a particular college for your child is to use the net price calculators. Every university and college in the country now must have a net price calculator accessible on its website, and the easiest way to find it is to search "name of college + net price calculator." The net price calculators will help you learn what it will cost your family for your student to attend that particular college, as each college or university will have slightly different methods for determining how much they will charge each particular student. In addition to this, some schools will meet full demonstrated financial need, while other schools will not. The schools that will not meet full demonstrated financial need are generally more expensive and leave students with more student loans to pay off.

The net price calculator is definitely a handy tool in figuring out which schools your child should apply to in the first place, since you can eliminate schools that will simply be too expensive. It's not a perfect method by any means though, as the calculators have many limitations:

- The price calculated is meant for first-time, full-time undergraduates.
- The financial aid package can also change quite a bit from year to year.
- It is not meant to determine out-of-state tuition for public schools.
- Many, possibly most, net price calculators do not take merit aid into account.
- Many net price calculators only allow the input of limited data, and therefore produce unreliable results. The best calculators ask for more detailed information.

### Merit Aid

This is the aid that is doled out to high-achieving students who may, but don't necessarily, qualify for need-based aid. It's important to realize that not all schools actually give merit aid, so check first if you're hoping for that bonus break in tuition.

The easiest way to find out if a school you're interested in offers merit aid is by searching "name of school + merit aid." You will usually be given a link to the financial section of a school's website and a list of what they offer. Some schools are incredibly generous and offer half or full-tuition merit aid. Some schools will have a few awards around $25,000, $10,000, and $5,000 per year. And some schools will only give around $1,000 or $2,000 per year to merit scholarship finalists. Therefore, it's important to find out, once you know if a school provides merit aid, how much they actually give.

Here's the catch: most highly selective schools don't offer merit aid because they don't need to. All their applicants are very high achieving, so they don't need to try to attract top applicants.

So, who does give merit aid? I have found that schools that accept fewer than 20-25% of their applicants rarely offer merit aid, and very few private schools on the east and west coasts offer merit aid. You are more likely to find merit aid at slightly less selective private schools. If you move away from the coasts, you are more likely to find more selective institutions offering merit aid there than you are at comparable schools on the coasts. If your child's qualifications are significantly higher than the middle 50% of applicants at a school that offers merit aid, then your child is more likely to at least be a candidate for the merit aid. The website Scholarships 360.org includes a list of colleges that offer merit aid. You can also view colleges with the highest percentages of students receiving merit aid on U.S. News and World Report. It is important to note that merit aid is usually figured into the financial aid package, not placed on top. So, if a student receives $10K in merit aid and was going to receive $20K in financial aid, the whole package may still be $20K as a combination of need and merit-based aid.

The above information is meant to be a good starting point to begin evaluating the costs of higher education. I recommend doing some of this research before your child falls in love with a particular school. Although you may choose to let them apply to a couple expensive schools anyway to "see what happens," it will save you and your child a lot of stress down the road if they mostly apply to schools they can love that are also affordable.

A wonderful resource that gives lots of in-depth information about the cost of college and how to plan is http://www.theCollegeSolution.com.

# CHAPTER 13

# WHO GETS MERIT SCHOLARSHIPS AND FOR HOW MUCH MONEY?

When discussions arise about paying for college, someone will inevitably mention scholarships. For the uninitiated, it seems to be a bit of a given that there's a lot of scholarship money out there for bright, motivated students. As a parent of a college-bound high school student, I set out to find out just what scholarships are actually out there, who gets them, and how much money can the students hope to get.

I began by consulting several free websites that list available scholarships such as: www.niche.com, www.cappex.com, www.unigo.com, www.fastweb.com, www.scholarships.com, www.collegeboard.com, and more. Many of these websites also offer other very useful information for parents and students regarding the college search process, so I recommend checking them out as they may be helpful.

The first thing to know is that there are hundreds, if not thousands, of scholarships out there. However, a quick search of them will show you that most scholarships are for 1 or 2K, some are renewable, and some are not. My son's high school guidance counselor said that on average, ten private scholarship applications yield one award. Most applications require filling out a form and writing an essay. Some require teacher recommendations and other materials. Some quick math shows that a student can put in a lot of work and receive nothing or a couple thousand dollars total. Therefore, it seems like a good idea to concentrate on scholarships that give more money and that aren't overwhelmingly competitive. Unfortunately, these are not necessarily easy to find.

## What Kinds of Scholarships are out there?

When I looked on the scholarship websites, it was clear that the overwhelming majority of available scholarships are for students with financial need or who come from underrepresented backgrounds. Girls, as a group, sometimes fit in this category, but if you are hoping to find a scholarship for a white, middle class boy, the pool of available scholarships really shrinks. I didn't find many scholarships at all that are solely based on academic talent or achievement, unless the student had really accomplished something incredible, such as win a national science competition.

## Specialized

I remember parents of older kids telling me there are so many different kinds of scholarships out there that there is something for everyone. I have not found that to be true. Although there are a number of scholarships for students who fall into very specific groups, many of the groups are really obscure. Most of them aren't for very much money so it might not be possible to accumulate much scholarship money unless you happen to fall into more than one of these very specific groups. Some examples of the eligibility for these scholarships are: children of federal employees, children of a parent with a disability, students who work as caddies, children that have overcome extreme adversity, child of an employee of a company such as Coca Cola, students who want a career in criminal justice, children or grandchildren of members of the Game Wardens Association, students who want to study entomology or environmental health nursing or broadcasting or work in the restaurant industry. I found several scholarships for youth bowlers. There is a scholarship local to my area for students interested in conservation who have a hunting license. As you can see, you may very well find a special interest scholarship for your child, but many kids will not fit in to any of the groups. My son is interested in birding and knot-tying and he's a vegetarian, and I could not find a thing for him.

## Essay and Project

The scholarships that seem to be available to everyone are the ones that reward a winning essay. The essay might be about an Ayn Rand novel where the student demonstrates a strong understanding of her philosophy—there are actually a few of these, and the student can win $10,000! I found another competition where the student can take part in an ecology project: http://www.wildernessproject.org/volunteer_apprentice_ecologist. This is pretty cool, but the award is only $1,000, and it's an awful lot of work: The student must conduct an environmental stewardship project, take photos of the project in action, write an essay about the project, and upload the photos and essay.

There is the prestigious Regeneron Science Talent Search that rewards students who conduct scientific research. The winner gets $250,000! But, 1,800 or so kids apply. There are 40 finalists that win at least $25,000, but that's only 2.5% of applicants, and they are impressive. You can read about them here: https://student.societyforscience.org/regeneron-sts-2018-top-ten

Needless to say, your research needs to be top notch to be considered. My son loves science and research, but his research project yielded inconclusive results, so he didn't even bother to enter.

### The Most Merit Aid

By all accounts, the most merit aid comes from the schools themselves. Some schools don't offer any merit aid, but many are very generous and will reward their top applicants—often without an additional application. There was a chat about this on CollegeConfidential.com several years ago.

You can read The U.S. News and World Report article with *"10 Colleges That Give Merit Aid to the Most Students"* (Powell, Farran, 2018) or on Time.com, *"The 46 Best Colleges for Getting Big Merit Scholarships"* (Clark, Kim, 2017). If you are interested in how academic merit aid works in colleges, this is article from Forbes is fantastic: *"Which Colleges Offer Big-Time Academic Merit Aid Money"* (Onink, Troy, 2015).

# SECTION 5 GETTING ORGANIZED

# CHAPTER 14
# MAKE A SPREADSHEET, OR TWO!

Some people love making spreadsheets. If you're one of them, then you will love this process! If you don't, do it anyway. It really helps organize the college search process. My son had two spreadsheets, one for the colleges he was considering and all the relevant information, and one for the activities he participated in throughout high school, including during the summers. The college spreadsheet makes it easier to see how many reach, target, and safety schools are on the list. It also allows you to include information about cost of attendance, application due dates, financial aid information, SAT scores the schools are looking for, and any other information you find important. The activity spreadsheet helps you keep track of hours spent on activities and duties performed. It can highlight growth in certain areas, or maybe show areas that could use improvement.

I've included samples below.

Sample College Search Spreadsheet Headers

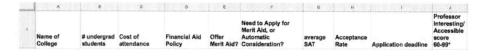

| Name of College | # undergrad students | Cost of attendance | Financial Aid Policy | Offer Merit Aid? | Need to Apply for Merit Aid, or Automatic Consideration? | average SAT | Acceptance Rate | Application deadline | Professor Interesting/ Accessible score 60-99* |
|---|---|---|---|---|---|---|---|---|---|

These headers are just examples—make sure to include information that's important and relevant to you. The last column, "Professors Interesting/Accessible," comes straight from the Princeton Guide and refers to how students at this institution view the quality of teaching at the school, and how available the professors are outside of class.

Sample Activity Spreadsheet Headers

| ACTIVITY | SUMMER ACTIVITY | WORK EXPERIENCE | VOLUNTEER EXPERIENCE | HOBBIES | YEARS/DATES INVOLVED | ROLE | DESCRIPTION OF ACTIVITY AND DETAILS ABOUT MY ROLE | HOURS SPENT PER WEEK/NUMBER OF WEEKS PER YEAR |
|---|---|---|---|---|---|---|---|---|

This spreadsheet could include another column to list achievements in the activities, or those could be listed in the "role," section.

# SECTION 6 APPLYING AND GETTING IN

## CHAPTER 15
## WHAT ARE SELECTIVE SCHOOLS LOOKING FOR?

For the most in-depth analysis ever, you should probably read the article, *"How to Get Into Harvard and the Ivy League, by a Harvard Alum,"* (Cheng, Allen, 2018), about what the few most selective colleges are looking for. The only problem with this article is its length, as it takes forever to read. If you don't have more than an hour, then read this chapter, and realize that my version is broader because I'm talking about all selective schools (accepting less than 30% of applicants), not just the handful of most selective ones (accepting less than 10%).

It is an endless source of confusion for most families: What on Earth are those selective schools looking for? Many parents and students trade horror stories of kids with perfect GPAs and test scores who didn't get into highly selective schools. I pored over college websites, books, webinars, and many online resources to learn more about the qualities selective schools are looking for. Note, I include the percentages of importance for each category based on numbers given by www.thecollegevine.com, but I have seen these numbers vary, and I've read on college websites themselves that they don't have a hard formula. Use the percentages as a guideline.

### Grades and Test Scores

It's no surprise that these are indeed important, but grades and test scores are not the whole picture. The GPA and test scores (SAT and/or ACT and SAT subject tests) combined count for about 30% of the application. What it means is that in addition to these scores, there will be many more factors weighed. You can think of these scores as a kind of gateway to being considered for admission at these highly selective schools. This is different from less selective schools, where certain GPA and test scores can guarantee admission.

GRADES: The schools will look not only at the grades, but also at the classes the applicant took. They are looking to see that the student took the most challenging courses available and excelled in them.

SAT/ACT: The SAT and ACT test scores are pretty straightforward. You can read about what the range of scores were for admitted students in previous years and see what is required to be considered for admission. If your student scores in the low range of test scores for admitted students, then other parts of his application must be very strong.

SAT Subject Tests: Many schools also require SAT subject tests. Those scores are a little less clear. Some scores can sound great, for example, a score of 780 (out of 800) on a subject test may sound amazing, until you learn that on the SAT II math subject test, that score only puts you in the 71st percentile. However, for the Literature subject test, a score of 780 puts you in the 96th percentile! It's really important to know what the scores mean. You can see the chart on the College Board website.

AP Exams: Everything I've read suggests that AP exams are not nearly as important for college admissions as the SAT and ACT. How the student did in the AP class itself is more important. AP exams scores are usually self-reported on college applications. It certainly doesn't hurt if a student has very high AP scores, and low scores can definitely be a red flag for colleges, particularly if the student received a high grade in the class. This could mean the high school the student attended practices grade inflation, which would reflect badly on the overall transcript. If a student has high AP exam scores, by all means include them. But if you have to choose whether to spend more time studying for AP exams or SAT subject tests, definitely spend the time preparing for the SAT subject tests.

## Extracurriculars

Once your grades and test scores have passed muster, selective colleges and universities really want to know how you spend your time. It makes sense. Learning about an applicant's activities helps them understand the student, learn about what they care about and how passionate they are, and how much time they devote to these activities.

According to the website www.thecollegevine.com, "Highly selective college are looking for students who will be successful at their institution, who will go on to be successful in life, and who will in turn make their school look good, so that they continue to keep their reputation as a highly selective school with top-notch students."

The most selective schools tend to look for a well-rounded student body, but not necessarily well-rounded students. They are looking for students with fewer activities, but who have been highly successful and focused in these activities. They are looking for leaders and achievers who have distinguished themselves. They are not looking for students who have just participated in activities. I found this very interesting. Many people have the impression that a student must play a sport or must join a particular kind of club. But this isn't true. If you're captain of the sports team, have won awards or broken records, then that is what they are looking for. If you're the president of the club, or started a new one, then that's what schools are looking for. Has the student won or achieved something on an international or national level? Schools are really impressed by that. Has the student accomplished something on a state or local level? That's awesome too. But joining a bunch of activities and just showing up once a week isn't really going to impress them. I will go more in detail about how to assess extracurricular activities in Chapter 16, "How Do Colleges Rank Extracurricular Activities?"

I actually think this is really good news for a student hoping to gain admission to a highly selective university. They don't want you to jump through a bunch of hoops just because it will look good. They are really looking for focused, passionate students who are doing things because they care about them. It doesn't hurt if you happen to be exceptionally talented either, of course, as those are the people who will be winning the math, music, and athletic competitions. But, there is plenty of room to shine for students who can lead or start groups and spend time doing what they love.

## Essays

The college essays are also really important and count for another 25% of the application, so students really don't want to wait until the last minute and rush these. Ideally, the essay will do a good job of creating a picture of the student. Overall, the college application should be viewed as a cohesive whole, a package that tells the story of the student. Hopefully the extracurricular activities and student's choice of classes will tell part of the story, and the essays are a great way to elaborate on these expressed interests and experiences. If the college review board can really get a feel for the student including his or her struggles, interests, and passions, then the student has a better chance of standing out as someone who will thrive at their institution.

## Letters of Recommendation

These count for roughly 15% of the overall application. Students should choose a teacher that knows him or her well and can speak to the student's strengths. The teacher should probably be from the student's junior year, since it's the most recent. A college may question why a student went back to sophomore year to find a teacher to write a recommendation. Usually students need a letter from a guidance counselor as well, so it's not a bad idea to try to set up appointments from time to time so the guidance counselor can get an idea of the student's strengths, interests, and goals. This is not always so easy as high school guidance counselors have an average of 482 students to get to know!

## Interview

The interview counts for just about 5% of the application process. Some schools value it over others, so it's important to do one if the school you want to attend recommends it. Some schools don't offer interviews at all. Apparently, interviews that take place on .campus will ultimately have greater value than off-site interviews with an alumnus. The interview's main purpose is to confirm what the rest of the application has already indicated, that yes, this student would be a great addition to our school. The interview can really only change the outcome in the admission process if it is a total disaster. I'm not sure what would need to occur during the interview for that to happen, but if it goes pretty well then that's probably good enough.

# CHAPTER 16

# HOW DO COLLEGES RANK EXTRACURRICULAR ACTIVITIES?

This chapter is mostly relevant for students seeking admission at highly selective colleges and universities. Many large, public universities do focus primarily on grades and test scores, and simply don't have the time or ability to do a "holistic review" of the college application, which would take extracurriculars and essays, etc. into account. However, I still think that understanding how the most selective schools view extracurriculars can be helpful for any applicant looking to put together the strongest application possible, and will give the applicant the most options when it's time to apply to college.

I've touched on how colleges, especially highly selective colleges, view extracurriculars in Chapter 15, *"What Are Selective Schools Looking For?"* and Chapter 6, *"Kids Feeding the Fire With Misinformation."* I thought I'd go more in-depth on this topic because it's so important for college applications. Many people are focused on the importance of grades and test scores on the college application, and then think that if you throw in participation in a sport or prestigious-sounding club it will almost certainly lead to admission at any college, including the most selective. But a little research will reveal that this is not true.

I've mentioned that I attended several webinars put on by www.thecollegevine.com, a student mentorship and college admissions consulting company (with a team who all attended Ivy League or similar tier schools). I've also referred several times to this article, *"How to Get Into Harvard and the Ivy League, by a Harvard Alum"* (Cheng, Allen, 2018). The information I learned from these sources was confirmed by the information sessions I attended with my son put on by MIT, Swarthmore, University of Chicago, University of Rochester, Grinnell, Carnegie Mellon, Cornell University and other schools. The same advice was given in the book, *The Enlightened College Applicant* (Belasco and Bergman, 2016). So, what are colleges looking for?

Colleges want students who are passionate about something. They are looking for students with unique talents and interests who have a record of accomplishment.

If you think about it, it makes sense. A passionate student who has focused on an area of interest and really accomplished something has already demonstrated success. This is someone who is likely to be driven, focused, and successful in college, and will go on to do wonderful things in life. These students will make their college look good and enhance its reputation. Extracurricular activities are all the things students do when they are not in school, and therefore reveal a lot about the student. So, how do colleges rate these activities? Please keep in mind that the below levels are my crude attempt to visually organize activities into neat groups. Many activities will fall outside these groups, and I don't think the college admissions review staff sit there with a chart when evaluating applications. This is meant to give an idea of different levels of accomplishment in different areas, and how the experts (see sources referred to above) have rated their value to colleges in the admissions process.

## Top Level
### (These accomplishments will be rare)
- Student won a national award
- Student is an athlete recruited to a Division 1 School
  Student is president or founder of an organization that has accomplished something of note on a national or international level
- Student is somehow otherwise acknowledged as the top in their activity or interest area

If this section makes you a little shaky, you are not alone! However, although I've seen similar information in several sources, I don't think most students have this level of accomplishment on their applications. But you can see why an applicant with this level of achievement (plus the grades, test scores, and good essays) could gain admittance anywhere he or she wanted to go! I think activities at this level pretty much blow the application reviewers away.

## Second Level
### (These accomplishment are also really impressive)
- Student is president or founder of an organization at local or state level

- Student is team captain for a sport, particularly if team wins at state level
- Student wins an award at the state level
- Student plays first chair instrument in local orchestra or band
- These students are still very accomplished and have proven leadership, but overall it's at a more local level than the top level.

### Third Level

- Smaller leadership role in an organization such as secretary or treasurer
  Student plays an instrument with some distinction, but not first chair
- Student plays a sport with some distinction
- Any activity where student has some leadership or shows some initiative.

### Fourth Level

- Student is a member of a team
- Student is a participant in a club
- Student plays a sport with no distinction
- Students takes music lessons
- Volunteer

It's pretty easy to see how and why colleges would regard the top two levels so highly. These are students who have really applied themselves, developed talents, pursued passions, and truly stand out. It can seem overwhelming to read these lists at first, but it is also enlightening. Every school information session we attended emphasized quality over quantity. They don't want to see a laundry list of where the student shows up to warm a seat. They would much prefer one, two, or three focused activities where the student has really applied herself and accomplished something.

Another message we've heard over and over is the importance of increasing involvement over time with an activity. Colleges want to see a progression over the course of high school.

I was surprised at first to see that general volunteering is valued so little on college applications. But I realized that it's another area where "anyone can do it." It's not that it looks bad on a college application, but many students exhaust themselves trying to log a lot of volunteer hours, often in unrelated activities, and it doesn't necessarily show passion or leadership or real accomplishment (although it can reveal a kind heart). This activity is like all the others though—if the student can show initiative, leadership, progress, and success with a particular volunteer activity, then colleges will value it.

Ideally this information will help demystify how colleges value and rate extracurricular activities. There aren't any activities that students "should" do, and students shouldn't try to do everything. The overwhelming message is to find an activity or two, get increasingly involved during high school, and take it as far as possible.

# CHAPTER 17

## HOW TO CRAFT THE COLLEGE ADMISSIONS ESSAY,
By Wendy Bellermann


The thing about a college essay is that your child will want to tell the admissions committee something wonderful about herself. She will want to talk about the soccer game in which victory was snatched from the jaws of defeat, and then talk about how she was changed. Or discuss her trip to Guatemala and how she learned about how much she has compared to others in this world. She will want to use sophisticated language and long sentences as if she's giving a speech, because that's what high school students do when they want to sound grown up and impressive.

### Tell a Story
The thing is, admissions committees have to read about a zillion essays in the time between November and April, and it's more important to catch their interest and attention, not by being impressive, but by being different and telling a story. Who wouldn't rather read a story than an essay? Your child's job in the essay is to make it more of a narrative and less of a school paper. How does she do this? She needs to start by choosing one of the prompts from the Common Application and deciding how she can shape it to her interests. Have her think about the qualities she's trying to evoke, then think of specific examples that show those qualities, and weave a story around that. The characteristic should be one that is broad enough that it can encompass aspects of her central nature, events in her life, and her future goals. From there, have her pick several anecdotes from her life that relate to that theme—you will want to have several so you don't get locked

in on one and then keep overworking it. You'll want three or four at this point.

For example, my daughter, Claire, chose the prompt "describe an aspect of yourself" and focused on her love of the natural world. She had been raising butterflies for fun, and linked that to her volunteer work with children at a nature camp, her interest in hiking, and her research on butterfly diseases. She took a hobby and turned it into a narrative about a person who is persistent, self-motivated, curious and quirky. She showed herself being those qualities through her actions, rather than by claiming them through words. At the end of her essay, she mentioned that she would like to major in biology and become a research biologist. So in her case, "aspect of self" => theme of nature => her core self, things she has done, and things she'd like to do with the help of the college.

## Brainstorm

Once your child has chosen some anecdotes, have her brainstorm on each one, focusing on SHOWING rather than TELLING. If she wants to demonstrate her stubbornness, don't write, "I'm the most stubborn person you'll ever meet," or "I consider stubbornness an important characteristic in someone who wants to succeed in business." Instead, write a list or loose scatter sheet of details about the moments she wants to talk about. Have her be specific, use all of her senses, integrate dialogue. Who was there? How did they react? How did you feel? What did people say? Ask her to imagine she is telling the story at a party—how would she set the scene? When she's told the story in real life, what bits do people react to most? Try to fill a sheet of paper for each anecdote. A sheet on stubbornness might look like: "boulder, climbing, stream, hawk, falling, knee on top, hands grabbing, everyone offering help, finally standing on top, easy to jump down." Even if she doesn't use each element, it's better to have them there now than wish she did later. Have her show herself in action. This period of writing should be very loose and casual. She should not be creating polished prose at all at this time—just setting out thoughts, details, story elements. After she is done brainstorming, have her look back over the papers and think of ways to link elements together.

## Refine Ideas

Once you have the brainstorms, have her think about how each anecdote does or does not illustrate the narrative she wants to convey. Does the one about the Girl Scout trip really illustrate her generosity and relate to her interest in pre-med, or would the one about getting out of the car in the driving rainstorm to help an injured dog do that better? Could she combine the two? ("The icy rain running down my sleeve was even more uncomfortable than the rocks I slept on after sharing my sleeping pad…").

Think also about mixing up the timeline. A story doesn't have to progress from beginning to end. It could start with the end ("last year I released 40 butterflies and presented my research at the NJ Entomological Society" [though really that would be better as "Presenting my research at the NJ Entomological Society, I was most proud of going from 5 to 40 butterflies and discovering the bacterium that was affecting them"]). It could start with the beginning ("My first year I only raised 5 butterflies, but when they flew away my heart lifted."). It could start in the middle ("The caterpillars kept turning to black goo late in the season. I was determined to know why."). Try to have your first sentence zero in on an element that demonstrates the central aspect or characteristic, but don't SAY what that is. "The sound of my trumpet echoed through Lincoln Center, past the place where my grandfather should have been standing," is better than "My determination has never paid off as much as it did when I played my trumpet at Lincoln Center."

### Write a Draft

After she has focused on her central characteristics, brainstormed on some anecdotes and thought about her structure, have her write a couple of drafts and speak them out loud. Ask questions—what happened next? Why did you decide to climb the hill? Why did you quit when you first studied trumpet? Help your child think about whether the story shows what she wants it to. If she is trying to show how fearless she is in asking questions, what questions specifically show how curious she is? And when, how often, under what circumstances? Did the teacher notice her trying to prove him wrong? What was the reaction of other students in the class when she asked all these questions? How did it feel to be the only one asking questions? If people seemed annoyed, then note what that felt like and continue with the story about asking questions—that SHOWS that she is fearless rather than having to say it outright.

### Revise and Edit

Once you have your anecdotes in rough draft form, have a new reader go through them so you can have a fresh perspective. What questions does the reader have? What central characteristic does she think the stories illustrate? Does one grab her attention more than the other? Does the draft paint a picture of someone who demonstrates the central theme? Are there bits that are boring, or tell rather than show? At this point, you might want to add in some framing devices like a quote at the end, or a mention of how college can help him achieve his dream of X, or how he wants to combine emphases on art and math to further his interest in Y.

The main goal of the essay is to grab the reader's attention through detail and illustrate the writer's character through detail. When the writer create a narrative structure that shows what kind of person she is, and how aspects of her life support that character, the admissions officer is more likely to remember her.

---

### Wendy Bellermann

Wendy worked in the writing labs at Colby College, where she earned her BA, and at SUNY Albany, where she attained her MA in composition. Wendy taught Writing Workshop (freshman English) for 5+ years at NYU, where she earned her MPhil. Wendy's daughter, Claire, was accepted to every college she applied to (partially, I'm sure, because of her excellent essays).

Wendy drew on her experience, and the editorial feedback of a college admissions counselor, to guide her daughter and write this piece.

---

A few more excellent resources for crafting the college admissions essay can be found in the resources section at the end of this book.

# CHAPTER 18

# DO COLLEGES RECRUIT FOR ACADEMICS?

Whether or not colleges recruit for academics is a source of confusion for many people. After all, once students enter sophomore or junior year of high school, postcards and emails start pouring in from colleges and universities all over the country (and some international schools too). Many are personalized with the student's first name, and some seem to know about the student's strengths and interests, "as a young writer you are probably wondering whether…." or "as a budding scientist you are probably looking for…" So, are these schools handpicking students they think of as strong candidates for their school? Have they sought out kids they hope will apply because they really want to admit them?

The short answer is no.

Here's the long answer: Admissions offices purchase student contact information. The lists may be based on general test scores, stated interests or intended major, or demographics, but it's still not personal. The blog post, *"Top 5 FAQs About All That College Mail"* (Fisher, Ian) does a good job explaining who receives literature from colleges, "College X might want the information for every student in the Western United States who scores between 50 and 70 on the reading section of the PSAT; University Y might ask for girls whose math scores exceed 30 on the ACT. In the end, a very small percentage of these students will turn into active prospects and even fewer will turn into real applicants. You're being targeted because you are from a certain demographic, but not because of who you are. They simply couldn't know details about your academic career at this point." Why do they do this? According to *"Why Colleges Aggressively Recruit Applicants Just to*

*Turn Them Down,*" (Colarusso, Laura, 2015) colleges will "recruit to deny." Colarusso wrote, "Even the most elite colleges, including those in the Ivy League, send letters encouraging many students to apply although, high-school counselors say, most of the students' odds of getting in are infinitesimal." She goes on to say, "Technological innovations—email being the biggest—let them make contact on a large scale at a low cost."

Schools want to have lots of kids apply because they get to reject more. This makes them more "selective," which raises their college ranking.

A student in New Jersey was so frustrated by this that she wrote a piece, "*Dear Elite Colleges, Please Stop Recruiting Students Like Me If You Know We Won't Get In*" (Graves, Amanda, 2014) for the Washington Post. She knew that her grades and test scores wouldn't get her into an elite school, yet she received solicitations from Yale, Harvard, and University of Chicago, among others. She wrote, "Naturally, I went to Google. I learned that each year, Yale courts not only me but roughly 79,999 other prospective students (down from 240,000 in 2005) for its class of 1,300. For the class of 2018, Yale rejected 93.7 percent of its applicants."

## Don't Dismay!

Does this mean they don't want you? Not necessarily—it's simply not personal. They don't know enough about you. Therefore, it is important that you find schools that are actually a match based on realistic assessments of grades, test scores, and extracurricular activities. If your student is in the low range in these areas based on previously admitted students, then this school is a reach. If you are not realistic, you might be very disappointed. As I mentioned in an earlier chapter, I know a young woman who applied to 13 colleges and was only accepted at one. She was devastated, and it was stressful for the whole family.

I have searched extensively and can find no examples of students recruited by colleges for academics (athletics is obviously a different story). Even in the cases of ridiculously accomplished young people like Jack Andraka: www.ivycoach.com/the-ivy-coach-blog/college-admissions/an-absurdly-remarkable-college-applicant/ who invented a new type of sensor to detect early-stage pancreatic cancer while still in high school, there is no evidence he was recruited by Stanford, or anywhere else, although I'm sure he had NO problem getting in everywhere he applied.

And for another student, Michael Brown: www.inc.com/bill-murphy-jr/this-brilliant-student-got-into-all-20-top-colleges-he-applied-to-by-doing-these-9-things.html, who is clearly what the Ivy Leagues schools are looking for and was accepted everywhere he applied, there is no evidence he was recruited.

So, when those emails and postcards start flowing in, take a look at them, make a list of schools you actually like that are a realistic fit, and don't be afraid to hit "delete," or fill up the recycle bin with the others that you realistically know you will never attend.

# CHAPTER 19

## DEMONSTRATED INTEREST

One question that comes up again and again for prospective college students and their parents is, "how important is demonstrated interest?"

Demonstrated interest is, to use the definition from, *"What 'Demonstrated Interest' Means in College Admissions,"* (Ross, Kelly Mae, 2018) in the U.S. News and World Report, "when prospective students show enthusiasm and curiosity about a school during the application process." You can show interest in a school in a number of ways. An interested student can tour the school and attend an information session. The student can attend an information session for that school in their local area or at a college fair. The student can sign up to be on the mailing list for that school, or sign up for an admissions interview (if the school offers them). The student can contact a professor or coach at the school, or otherwise make specific inquiries at the admissions office. Apparently, according to the U.S. News and World Report, even opening the emails sent out by the school can help, as some schools have software that can track who opens them.

But how important is it? From my own experience attending information sessions, it depends on the school. When we visited the University of Rochester, they made it clear that demonstrated interest is very important. They want students to reach out to them, and they highly recommend that students sign up for an admissions interview. Other schools, such as Carnegie Mellon and Emory University, make it clear that they don't care about demonstrated interest. Furthermore, Carnegie Mellon explicitly states in their mailed marketing materials that they do not want to be bombarded with calls and inquiries. Many of these schools have changed their policies. Emory used to actively encourage demonstrated interest. Other schools suggest that the application essay on why you want to attend the school is the best way to show interest. Applying early action or early decision is another way to show interest.

For schools that care about demonstrated interest, the main reason is because they want to ensure a higher yield (the percentage of students from the admitted pool of applicants who actually attend the school). In a broad sense, schools that have no problem getting their admitted applicants to enroll don't seem to care much about demonstrated interest, whereas schools that often lose admitted applicants to more prestigious schools seem to care more. This makes sense. If there are two similar applicants, and one has shown a great interest in a school and one hasn't, it would make sense to admit the applicant who seems more likely to enroll.

Since so much of the college search and application process can be time-consuming, the idea of discovering which schools do and don't care about demonstrated interest can seem overwhelming. In "*A Lesson In Demonstrated Interest,*" (Montgomery, Mark), Montgomery suggests contacting specific colleges to see if they care about demonstrated interest. This seems like a pretty good idea for a student's top choice schools (it would be a lot of work to do this for 20 schools). The good news is that by going through the college search process, most students do demonstrate interest by visiting schools, getting on mailing lists, and attending local information sessions for schools they can't visit. For top choices, it is a good idea to see if the school recommends an interview.

One misperception I've come across is that demonstrated interest can help an applicant that might not otherwise meet the academic requirements a school is looking for. I have not come across anything to support this claim. In the blog post, "*Does Demonstrated Interest Matter in College*

*Admissions?*" (Madden, Stephen, 2018), Madden interviewed Jessica Hess, an admissions director who has worked at several schools who said, "of course, sending emails to professors and going to see the school rep at college fairs alone isn't going to get anybody into college. You need grades, extracurriculars, and test scores. The real value of demonstrated interest, says Hess, is that it offers one more way to help tell good candidates apart." She likened the college admissions process to dating, where the student and school must be a good match.

If you and your student make an effort to find schools that really fit in terms of a student's abilities, interests, and goals, then you will naturally demonstrate interest when you attend information sessions, request more information, or visit campus. Finding the right schools can be a lot of fun. And, as my friend Melissa pointed out, it's important to remember to keep the process fun.

# CHAPTER 20

# DO FAST APPLICATIONS MEAN COLLEGES WANT YOU?

During the summer before and early in the fall of the senior year of high school, many students will receive offers from colleges to bypass the regular application process and use a streamlined application instead. The application fee or essays might be waived. Often the offer to use the fast application will come with flattery telling the student who he or she is just the type of high-achieving student they are looking for, and the names of the applications often have alluring titles with words such as "VIP" in them. So, does receiving one of these applications mean the college really wants you? Unfortunately, it seems it does not.

These fast applications were developed by a company called Royall & Co. According the article *"Colleges Market Easy, No-Fee Sell to Applicants,"* (Steinberg, Jacques, 2010) in The New York Times, "Royall helps each college identify potential applicants by buying lists of high school students' names and addresses from the College Board, based on how they performed on the PSAT or SAT, or on information they provided on their high school class rank, interests or ethnicity." While this might seem like a great way for colleges to find candidates they want, Steinberg wrote, "Marquette, with a freshman class of about 1,950, sent out about 40,000 of its 'Advantage' applications last year [2009], and will reject about 40 percent of its applicants over all." Obviously, they can't offer admission to most of the students they woo with the fast application, but the result is that they get more applicants.

According to Steinberg, the U.S. News and World Report "puts a premium on big jumps in applications, as well as in applicants' standardized test scores, in assembling its annual rankings." So, a big increase in applicants can mean a rise in rankings on U.S. News and World Report. This may seem like a cynical view, but in *"Fast Applications: What to Do When a College Gives You the VIP Treatment,"* (Bergman, Dave, 2014) Bergman wrote, it's just plain fact, "Many in the industry feel that fast apps cheapen the process and are a blatant attempt to drum up applicants in order to continue feeding the rankings beast." Few college admissions officials even bother to refute this characterization—that's pretty much just what they are." In *"Don't be Fooled By Priority Applications,"* (O'Shaughnessy, Lynn), O'Shaughnessy confirmed this, "For starters, it boosts their applications numbers. With the help of outside firms, colleges send out thousands and even tens of thousands of applications that are easier for teenagers to complete than the typical ones...Just because a student receives one of these applications certainly doesn't mean the school is interested in him or her. In some cases, schools use these applications to increase their applications so they can reject more students. Selectivity, after all, is something that US News' college rankings care about."

Ursinus College comes up in various articles as having been successful at this practice. Because of the priority application, they received more than double the number of applicants in one year, and then increased their applicant pool significantly more within the next two years. However, according to Steinberg, "every year Ursinus received more of Royall's "fast track" applications and offered admission to more applicants, but the percentage that accepted the offer—known as the yield—went down steadily." The university's vice president of enrollment ultimately felt uneasy with this "shaky foundation" and eventually stopped the practice.

There does not appear to be any real advantage to using the fast applications at all. As Bergman wrote, "VIP status in the application process in no way suggests that you will receive a large helping of merit aid. In fact, they don't even guarantee admission."

However, once armed with this information, I think it makes sense to use these applications to your advantage. By all accounts, the colleges using the fast applications give them the same consideration as the other applications they accept. It doesn't make sense to apply to schools you weren't already considering, since you won't have increased chances for financial aid or admission. But for colleges you were going to apply to anyway, if they offer to waive an essay or application fee and if you find the process easier, why not use it?

# RESOURCES

In the introduction I mentioned that I did a lot of research when going through the college search process with my oldest son. I am still doing a lot of research! It would be fair to say that I became and remain obsessed with the college search process, especially since we will have to go through all of this again in a few years with my younger son. After all, college is expensive! There are so many different kinds! It's four years of a student's life that you hope will set them on a good path to their future. You want your child to thrive. Who doesn't want to make the most informed decision possible when looking to send a child off to a four-year institution that could cost nearly $300,000? Although most families won't pay that, many students do end up with crushing amounts of debt.

I thought I'd share here some of my go-to resources for information which are the same resources I consulted for this book. Each one has a different focus and strengths, and that's why I decided to try to compile some of the most useful information here. For a full list of all the materials researched to write this book, please see the bibliography.

## WEB SITES

**College Confidential: http://www.collegeconfidential.com**
I can get lost in this site for hours. It's the kind of site where you can ask questions such as, "should I go to school x or school y?" or, "What kind of students go to school x?" and you will most likely have one or more threads pop up where people have weighed in on that exact question. You need to be careful and make sure that the people expressing their opinions actually have REAL INFORMATION and are not just repeating stereotypes or have a bone to pick, but many people who respond do attend a school mentioned in the question, or have a child that does. It can be useful for anecdotal information.

**The College Solution: http://www.thecollegesolution.com**
This site is run by Lynn O'Shaughnessy and she provides lots of information to help families make informed choices about college, usually focusing on finding affordable options. Lots of great financial advice here. She offers free webinars, a class you can pay for with more in-depth information, and loads of blog posts on pertinent topics on her web site.

**The College Vine: https://www.collegevine.com**
When I subscribed to US News and World Report, I was offered free webinars to attend put on by this group. They mostly focused on how to get in to elite colleges, but the advice was useful for all college applicants. They offer mentoring and SAT/ACT prep services for a fee. They offer webinars on topics such as, "How Ivy League Admissions Work"

**Niche.com: https://www.niche.com/colleges/search/best-colleges/**
This is a wonderful go-to site to get good information about specific colleges. You can see how schools are ranked in different areas of study, and find out about the GPA and test scores needed to get in. You can also see how students describe the other students at the school, the school as a whole, and how they view their professors. There are also individual student reviews.

**Unigo: https://www.unigo.com**
This site seems to offer a variety of services, but what I like is the section where students review the schools they're attending using a variety of criteria. Once again, you need to be careful how much value you put in any one particular rating, but I like to look for trends. Do many students complain about a lack of support from the administration? Do most of the students from a particular school seem to lack basic grammar skills? You get the idea.

**US News and World Report Best Colleges:
https://www.usnews.com/best-colleges**
This site needs to be taken with a grain of salt. It is helpful to see the "rankings" of schools to find out how "good" they are, and it is also helpful to see how these schools compare to others in specific majors and areas of study. This site comes under a lot of criticism because of how it ranks the schools and seems to motivate schools to use shady methods to increase their rankings, such as encouraging many students, even those without a chance of getting in, to apply, so that they can be rejected, and therefore make the school more selective. That said, there really is a lot of information here and it can be a helpful overall guide. If you get a subscription, you will also be notified about free webinars you can take that are often on very helpful topics regarding the college admissions process.

## FINANCIAL AID, SCHOLARSHIPS AND MERIT AID

Estimated Family Contribution (EFC) Calculator:
https://bigfuture.collegeboard.org/pay-for-college/paying-your-

share/expected-family-contribution-calculator

Information about the Estimated Family Contribution (EFC) from the Free Application for Federal Student Aid (FAFSA) website: https://fafsa.ed.gov/help/fftoc01g.htm

Scholarships 360 is a website with a list of colleges that offer merit aid: https://scholarships360.org/great-schools-great-scholarships-top-merit-scholarship-awards/

You can also view colleges with most percentages of students receiving merit aid on U.S. News and World Report: https://www.usnews.com/best-colleges/rankings/most-merit-aid

Clark, Kim. (2017, August 16). *The 46 Best Colleges for Getting Big Merit Scholarships*. Retrieved from http://time.com/money/4894643/best-colleges-merit-aid-scholarships/

Onink, Troy. (2015, May 31). *Which Colleges Offer Big-Time Academic Merit Aid Money*. Retrieved from https://www.forbes.com/sites/troyonink/2015/05/31/which-colleges-offer-big-time-academic-merit-aid-money/#6cea85924e28

Onink, Troy. (2015, May 31). *Estimating Your Eligibility For College Merit Aid Money*. Retrieved from https://www.forbes.com/sites/troyonink/2015/05/31/estimating-your-eligibility-for-college-merit-aid-money/#6aed9b491373

Powell, Farran. (2018, November 20) *12 Colleges That Give Merit Aid to the Most Students*. Retrieved from https://www.usnews.com/education/best-colleges/the-short-list-college/articles/2017-10-24/10-colleges-that-give-merit-aid-to-the-most-students

Lists of Scholarships: www.niche.com, www.cappex.com, www.unigo.com, www.fastweb.com, www.scholarships.com, www.collegeboard.com

You can find unusual scholarships on Scholarships.com: https://www.scholarships.com/financial-aid/college-scholarships/scholarships-by-type/weird-scholarships/

Ecology Scholarships: http://www.wildernessproject.org/volunteer_apprentice_ecologist

Regeneron Science Talent Search:
https://student.societyforscience.org/regeneron-sts-2018-top-ten


## COLLEGE GUIDES

Belasco, Andrew; Bergman, Dave. 2016. *The Enlightened College Applicant: A New Approach to the Search and Admissions Process.* Lanham, MD: Rowman & Littlefield.
This is a wonderful book. I suggest that everyone embarking on the college search process add it to their library. It demystifies the college application process by breaking it apart in small pieces and explaining what is important and what is not. There is a ton of research backing all their claims.

Fiske, Edward B., 2017. *Fiske Guide to Colleges*, 2018. Naperville, Ill: Sourcebooks, Inc.
This is my favorite all-purpose college guide. It covers only about 300 out of the more than 2,000 colleges and universities in the country, and it seems to leave out some very good options. That said, it shares helpful information about each institution such as admission requirements, most popular majors, size and male/female ratio, etc. It also has helpful descriptions of the academics and student life, and a list of schools that applicants to this school also like. Each year they come out with a new edition.

Franek, Robert; O'Toole, Karen; Soto, David. 2017. *The Princeton Review: The Best 382 Colleges.* New York: Penguin Randomhouse, LLC.
This is similar to the Fiske Guide. It covers more schools than the Fiske Guide, and gives exact information about cost of tuition, room, and board, unlike the Fiske Guide which just gives ranges. Although there is a lot of overlap with the Fiske Guide, each guide covers information that the other lacks, so I find it helpful to have both for cross-referencing. Many libraries carry both guides, so it's worth checking them out first to see how they work for you.

Greene, Howard, MA, M ed; Greene, Matthew, PhD. 2016. *The Hidden Ivies: 63 of America's Top Liberal Arts Colleges and Universities.* New York: HarperCollins.
I really like this book. It has very in-depth information about 63 private liberal arts colleges and universities. Although it's a limited number of schools, the information given about each school is so helpful in finding out specifically why it is special and stands out. Most of the schools are well-known, but we did learn about several schools we weren't familiar with

before that sound really great. There is also a lot of other helpful information in this book, including a section on writing college essays.

Pope, Loren. 2012. *Colleges That Change Lives: 40 Schools That Will Change the Way You Think About Colleges.* Penguin Books.
This is good and very different from The Hidden Ivies in that it focuses on B students. Pope highlights great liberal arts schools that may not be well-known, but offer great educations, access to professors, and opportunities. A refreshing perspective.

## COLLEGE RANKINGS

Money Magazine College Rankings: *These are the 727 Best Colleges in America.* (2018, August 13) http://time.com/money/best-colleges/

U.S. News & World Report: https://www.usnews.com/best-colleges

## HOW TO WRITE COLLEGE ADMISSIONS ESSAY

Paskova, Yana. (2017, August 2). *How to Conquer the Admissions Essay.* Retrieved from
https://www.nytimes.com/2017/08/02/education/edlife/college-application-essay-admissions.html,

McCammon, Ellen. (2016, November 19). *The 13 Best College Essay Tips to Craft a Stellar Application.*
Retrieved from https://blog.prepscholar.com/best-college-essay-tips

College Board. *8 Tips for Crafting Your Best College Essay.* Retrieved from https://bigfuture.collegeboard.org/get-in/essays/8-tips-for-crafting-your-best-college-essay

## COLLEGE MAIL

College Coach. *Top 5 FAQs About All That College Mail.* Retrieved from http://blog.getintocollege.com/top-5-faqs-about-all-that-college-mail/The blog

Colarusso, Laura M. (2015, January 12). *From the Hechinger Report. Why colleges aggressively recruit applicants just to turn them down.* Retrieved from https://www.pbs.org/newshour/education/colleges-ratchet-recruiting-applicants-just-turn

Graves, Amanda. (2014, November 17). *Dear elite colleges, please stop recruiting students like me if you know we won't get in.* Retrieved from https://www.washingtonpost.com/posteverything/wp/2014/11/17/dear-elite-colleges-please-stop-recruiting-students-like-me-if-you-know-we-wont-get-in/?noredirect=on&utm_term=.78dcbcc2bc8a


## DEMONSTRATED INTEREST

Mongomery, Mark. (2017). *A Lesson In Demonstrated Interest.* Retrieved from https://greatcollegeadvice.com/a-lesson-in-demonstrated-interest/

Madden, Stephen. (2018, July 20). *Does Demonstrated Interest Matter in College Admissions?*
Retrieved from https://blog.collegevine.com/does-demonstrated-interest-matter-in-college-admissions/

Empowerly Team. (2017, September 20). *Does Demonstrated Interest Matter for College Admissions?* Retrieved from http://blog.synocate.com/does-demonstrated-interest-matter-for-college-admissions

Ross, Kelly Mae. (2018, May 21). *What 'Demonstrated Interest' Means in College Admissions.* Retrieved from https://www.usnews.com/education/best-colleges/articles/2018-05-21/what-demonstrated-interest-means-in-college-admissions


## FAST APPLICATIONS

Steinberg, Jacques. (2011, February 14). *A College Opts Out of the Admissions Arms Race.* Retrieved from https://thechoice.blogs.nytimes.com/2011/02/14/ursinus/

Bergman, Dave. (2014, August 6). *"Fast" Applications: What to do when a college gives you the VIP treatment.* Retrieved from https://www.collegetransitions.com/blog/fast-apps/

O'Shaughnessy, Lynn. *Don't Be Fooled by Priority Applications.* Retrieved from http://www.thecollegesolution.com/dont-be-fooled-by-priority-applications/

Steinberg, Jacques. (2010, January 25). *Colleges Market Easy, No-Fee Sell to Applicants.* Retrieved from
https://www.nytimes.com/2010/01/26/education/26admit.html

# BIBLIOGRAPHY

Adams, Susan. *The Universities that Produce the Most CEO's.* Retrieved from https://www.forbes.com/sites/susanadams/2013/09/25/the-universities-that-produce-the-most-ceos/#5a5573b96262

Belasco, Andrew; Bergman, Dave. 2016. *The Enlightened College Applicant: A New Approach to the Search and Admissions Process.* Lanham, MD: Rowman & Littlefield.

Bergman, Dave. (2014, August 6). *"Fast" Applications: What to do when a college gives you the VIP treatment.* Retrieved from https://www.collegetransitions.com/blog/fast-apps/

Brewer, Emma. (2018, October 19). *Letter of Recommendation for a Basic Male MFA Applicant.* Retrieved from https://www.mcsweeneys.net/articles/letter-of-recommendation-for-a-basic-male-mfa-applicant?fbclid=IwAR2mhzGGGOHkWACFudNasMhEgLdVinLsObQB-hOkWdoyu9ZAf0XnakZehvE

Cheng, Allen. (2018, July 24). *How To Get Into Harvard and the Ivy League,* by a Harvard Alum. Retrieved from https://blog.prepscholar.com/how-to-get-into-harvard-and-the-ivy-league-by-a-harvard-alum

Clark, Kim. (2017, July 10). *How Money Ranked the 2017 Best Colleges.* Retrieved from http://time.com/money/4846386/how-money-ranks-best-colleges-2017/

Colarusso, Laura M. (2015, January 12). From the Hechinger Report. *Why colleges aggressively recruit applicants just to turn them down.* Retrieved from https://www.pbs.org/newshour/education/colleges-ratchet-recruiting-applicants-just-turn

College Coach. *Top 5 FAQs About All That College Mail.* Retrieved from http://blog.getintocollege.com/top-5-faqs-about-all-that-college-mail/The blog

College Board. *8 Tips for Crafting Your Best College Essay.* Retrieved from https://bigfuture.collegeboard.org/get-in/essays/8-tips-for-crafting-your-best-college-essay

College Board: *SAT Subject Test Percentile Ranks:* Retrieved from
https://secure-media.collegeboard.org/sat/pdf/sat-subject-tests-percentile-
ranks.pdf

DuBro, Olivia. (2015, Septmber 20). *Are honor societies still honorable?*
Retrieved from https://lhslance.org/2015/opinion/are-honor-societies-
still-honorable/

Easterbrook, Gregg. (2004, October 1). *Who Needs Harvard?* Retrieved from
https://www.brookings.edu/articles/who-needs-harvard/

Empowerly Team. (2017, September 20). *Does Demonstrated Interest Matter for
College Admissions?* Retrieved from
http://blog.synocate.com/does-demonstrated-interest-matter-for-college-
admissions

Finegold, Sam. (2013, December 9). *Harvard Undergrads are Teaching Each
Other and Harvard Doesn't Want to Talk About It.* Retrieved from
http://harvardpolitics.com/harvard/harvard-undergraduates-teaching-
harvard-doesnt-want-talk/

Fiske, Edward B., 2017. *Fiske Guide to Colleges*, 2018. Naperville, Ill:
Sourcebooks, Inc.

Franek, Robert; O'Toole, Karen; Soto, David. 2017. *The Princeton Review: The
Best 382 Colleges.* New York: Penguin Randomhouse, LLC.

Goldfarb, Zachary A. (2014, March 5). *These four charts show how the SAT
favors rich, educated families.* Retrieved from
https://www.washingtonpost.com/news/wonk/wp/2014/03/05/these-
four-charts-show-how-the-sat-favors-the-rich-educated-
families/?noredirect=on&utm_term=.2c07ab58ba77

Graves, Amanda. (2014, November 17). *Dear elite colleges, please stop recruiting
students like me if you know we won't get in.* Retrieved from
https://www.washingtonpost.com/posteverything/wp/2014/11/17/dear-
elite-colleges-please-stop-recruiting-students-like-me-if-you-know-we-wont-
get-in/?noredirect=on&utm_term=.78dcbcc2bc8a

Greene, Howard, MA, M ed; Greene, Matthew, PhD. 2016. *The Hidden Ivies:
63 of America's Top Liberal Arts Colleges and Universities.* New York:
HarperCollins.

The Ivy Coach website https://www.ivycoach.com/

Lanzat, Myelle and Kiersz, Andy. (2018, November 19). *The 50 Most Underrated Colleges in America.* Retrieved from https://www.businessinsider.com/most-underrated-colleges-in-america-2018-11

Leonhardt, David. (2011, February 21). *Revisiting the Value of Elite Colleges.* Retrieved from https://economix.blogs.nytimes.com/2011/02/21/revisiting-the-value-of-elite-colleges/

Kiersz, Andy. (2018, November 17). *Here's How We Ranked the Most Underrated Colleges In America.* Retrieved from https://www.businessinsider.com/most-underrated-colleges-in-america-methodology-sources-2018-11

Kretzschmar, Michelle. *50-50 Highlights: Colleges Producing the Most PhD Degree Recipients.* Retrieved from http://www.diycollegerankings.com/50-50-highlights-colleges-producing-the-most-students-receiving-phds/11028/

Krueger, Alan B. (2000, April 27). *Economic Scene; Children smart enough to get into elite schools may not need to bother.* Retrieved from https://www.nytimes.com/2000/04/27/business/economic-scene-children-smart-enough-get-into-elite-schools-may-not-need-bother.html

Madden, Stephen. (2018, July 20). *Does Demonstrated Interest Matter in College Admissions?* Retrieved from https://blog.collegevine.com/does-demonstrated-interest-matter-in-college-admissions/

McCammon, Ellen. (2016, November 19). *The 13 Best College Essay Tips to Craft a Stellar Application.* Retrieved from https://blog.prepscholar.com/best-college-essay-tips

Mongomery, Mark. (2017). *A Lesson In Demonstrated Interest.* Retrieved from https://greatcollegeadvice.com/a-lesson-in-demonstrated-interest/

MIT Admissions: *What to do in High School.* Retrieved from https://mitadmissions.org/apply/prepare/highschool/

Money Magazine College Rankings: *These are the 727 Best Colleges in America.* (2018, August 13) http://time.com/money/best-colleges/

Mulhere, Kaitlin. (2016, June 14). *Top Ten Colleges of Fortune 500 CEOs.* Retrieved from http://time.com/money/4364104/top-colleges-fortune-500-ceos/

Niche.com. 2019. *Colleges with the Best Professors in America.* Retrieved from https://www.niche.com/colleges/search/best-college-professors/

Niche.com. 2019. *Colleges with the Best Professors Methodology.* Retrieved from https://about.niche.com/methodology/best-college-professors/

Onink, Troy. (2015, May 31). *Estimating Your Eligibility For College Merit Aid Money.* Retrieved from https://www.forbes.com/sites/troyonink/2015/05/31/estimating-your-eligibility-for-college-merit-aid-money/#6aed9b491373

Onink, Troy. (2015, May 31). *Which Colleges Offer Big-Time Academic Merit Aid Money.* Retrieved from https://www.forbes.com/sites/troyonink/2015/05/31/which-colleges-offer-big-time-academic-merit-aid-money/#6cea85924e28

O'Shaughnessy, Lynn. *The Best High School Extracurriculars.* Retrieved from http://www.thecollegesolution.com/advice-on-high-school-extracurriculars/

O'Shaughnessy, Lynn. *The Colleges Where PhD's Get Their Start.* Retrieved from http://www.thecollegesolution.com/the-colleges-where-phds-get-their-start/

O'Shaughnessy, Lynn. *Don't Be Fooled by Priority Applications.* Retrieved from http://www.thecollegesolution.com/dont-be-fooled-by-priority-applications/

O'Shaughnessy, Lynn. *Don't Pay $280,000 for a bachelor's degree.* Retrieved from http://www.thecollegesolution.com/would-you-pay-28000-for-a-bachelors-degree/

O'Shaughnessy, Lynn. *!5 Things to Know About U.S. News' College Rankings.* Retrieved from http://www.thecollegesolution.com/15-things-to-know-about-u-s-news-college-rankings/

O'Shaughnessy, Lynn. *Looking for Great College Bargains.* Retrieved from http://www.thecollegesolution.com/looking-for-great-college-bargains/

O'Shaughnessy, Lynn. (2010, September 3). *Top 50 Schools That Produce Science PhDs.* Retrieved from https://www.cbsnews.com/news/top-50-schools-that-produce-science-phds/

Paskova, Yana. (2017, August 2). *How to Conquer the Admissions Essay.* Retrieved from https://www.nytimes.com/2017/08/02/education/edlife/college-application-essay-admissions.html,

Payscale.com. *College Salary Report:* https://www.payscale.com/college-salary-report

Payscale.com. *Best Schools for Majors.* Retrieved from https://www.payscale.com/college-salary-report/best-schools-by-majors

Pope, Loren. 2012. *Colleges That Change Lives: 40 Schools That Will Change the Way You Think About Colleges.* Penguin Books.

PrepScholar: https://www.prepscholar.com/

Princeton Admissions: *Helpful Tips.* Retrieved from https://admission.princeton.edu/how-apply/helpful-tips

Robinovitz, Judi. *The 10 Most Important Factors in College Admissions.* Retrieved from https://www.collegeexpress.com/counselors-and-parents/college-counselors/articles/articles-college-counselors/10-most-important-factors-college-admissions/

Ross, Kelly Mae. (2018, July 10). *11 Colleges Where Graduates Pursue Continuing Education.* Retrieved from https://www.usnews.com/education/best-colleges/the-short-list-college/articles/colleges-where-graduates-pursue-continuing-education

Ross, Kelly Mae. (2018, May 21). *What 'Demonstrated Interest' Means in College Admissions.* Retrieved from https://www.usnews.com/education/best-colleges/articles/2018-05-21/what-demonstrated-interest-means-in-college-admissions

Steinberg, Jacques. (2011, February 14). *A College Opts Out of the Admissions Arms Race.* Retrieved from https://thechoice.blogs.nytimes.com/2011/02/14/ursinus/

Steinberg, Jacques. (2010, January 25). *Colleges Market Easy, No-Fee Sell to Applicants.* Retrieved from
https://www.nytimes.com/2010/01/26/education/26admit.html

Townsend, Robert B. (2005, September 1). *Privileging History: Trends in the Undergraduate Origins of History PhDs.* Retrieved from
https://www.historians.org/publications-and-directories/perspectives-on-history/september-2005/privileging-history-trends-in-the-undergraduate-origins-of-history-phds

U.S. News & World Report: https://www.usnews.com/best-colleges

White, Gillian. (2015, August 17). *Does Going to a Selective College Matter?* Retrieved from
https://www.theatlantic.com/business/archive/2015/08/does-college-matter/400898/

Williams, Terry. (2018, October 11). *America's Top CEOs and their College Degrees.* Retrieved from
https://www.investopedia.com/articles/professionals/102015/americas-top-ceos-and-their-college-degrees.asp

Xu. (2014, March 1). *Why You Should (and Should Not) Join an Honors Society.* Retrieved from http://undergrad.osu.edu/buckeyes_blog/?p=11474